AWESOME OVER 50

*Fifty Ways to Embrace this
Chapter of your Life*

Heather Hyde

Copyright © 2020 Heather Hyde
ISBN: 9798554836459
All rights reserved.

*This book is dedicated to all the
Awesome Ones over 50
who would like to experience
this chapter of their life
as the most
fulfilling, exciting and memorable!*

CONTENTS

Introduction i

Chapter ONE   **1**
Re-Discover your YOUTHFUL SPIRIT

Tip #1   Go out and PLAY   3

Tip #2   Make up a FUN LIST   6

Tip #3   Have something to LOOK FORWARD TO   10

Tip #4   LEARN new things   14

Tip #5   Sometimes LAUGHTER IS THE BEST MEDICINE   19

Tip #6   THINK YOU'RE YOUTHFUL and you are!   23

Chapter TWO   **27**
FOCUS ON A LIVING PLAN *not* an Exit Plan

Tip #7   Re-Tirement or RE-HIREMENT?   29

Tip #8   Ignore the OLD-PERSON LABELS   33

Tip #9   Start your VISION BOARD   36

Tip #10   DON'T LOOK BACK… it could be a trap   41

Tip #11 FRAPPICCINOS, TAPAS & SUSHI, Oh My!!!	46

Chapter THREE 53
RE-JUVENATE & RE-CHARGE

Tip #12 Be a MOVER	55
Tip #13 ...and a SHAKER	60
Tip #14 These boots are made for WALKING	64
Tip #15 You look MARVELOUS	69
Tip #16 SELF-CARE is *not* Self-ish	74
Tip #17 One or two day GET-AWAYS	79

Chapter FOUR 85
Defying BIRTH CERTIFICATE DATES

Tip #18 What if there NEVER WAS A BIRTH CERTIFICATE?	87
Tip #19 It's your party... WEAR WHAT YOU WANT TO	90
Tip #20 Are you FEELING INVISIBLE?	94
Tip #21 Your superpower is YOUR CONFIDENCE	99

Chapter FIVE   103
Un-Stuck THE RUT

Tip #22	Find your AUTHENTIC SELF	105
Tip #23	KEEPING UP with The Joneses	114
Tip #24	The DOWNSIZING dilemma	117
Tip #25	Remember to TRUST YOUR INSTINCTS	122
Tip #26	When FOMO creeps in (fear of missing out)	127
Tip #27	Embracing the WARP SPEED WORLD	131

Chapter SIX   137
HEAL the Wounds

Tip #28	FORGIVENESS frees you	139
Tip #29	Don't give up on LOVE	146
Tip# 30	You are worthy of RESPECT	152
Tip #31	STRESS & WORRY are silent killers	158
Tip #32	Learn to truly RELAX	163

Chapter SEVEN   **171**
Wrinkles are your STORY-LINES

Tip #33	Talk PRO-AGE instead of Anti-Age	173
Tip #34	Ignore the NAY-SAYERS	177
Tip #35	Why not ditch THE DYE?	183
Tip #36	Born to be ME	188

Chapter EIGHT   **193**
You're never too old to DREAM

Tip #37	It's the JOURNEY, not the destination	195
Tip #38	See it, then BELIEVE IT	199
Tip #39	Find the TIME	204
Tip #40	Start the PROCESS	208
Tip #41	History proves AGE IS NOT A BARRIER	212
Tip #42	There's ALWAYS SOMETHING	215
Tip #43	NO EXPIRY DATE on dreams	219

Chapter NINE — 225
WHAT'S NEXT?!

Tip #44	The best things in life are not THINGS	227
Tip #45	Keep EVOLVING	232
Tip #46	Your EXPERIENCES HAVE VALUE	236
Tip #47	WHO ELSE is with you?	241
Tip #48	LOVE LIKE a person in their 90s…don't wait	247
Tip #49	Embrace an ATTITUDE OF GRATITUDE	251
Tip #50	… and finally - KEEP IT AWESOME!	255

INTRODUCTION

Welcome to OUR book! I say OUR book because if you're over 50, we're on this journey together.

Many of you are familiar with my YouTube videos and social media posts cheering on the chapter of life that I affectionately call, "Awesome over 50." My goal has always been to inspire others *of a certain age* to embrace the over-50 journey and I've been doing this for many years now.

I am truly appreciative of the viewer community that has grown, and continues to grow. I want to take this opportunity to say *thanks* to those who have engaged with my videos with millions of views. However, I was only able to scratch the surface of what I wanted to express with those short videos and social media posts, so this book became my vision and passion. It is my hope that this book offers you much more, through easy-to-read tips and encouragement while you're on this over-50 journey.

As I wrote this book, I poured my heart and soul into the process. It took me over a year of writing, re-writing, editing and re-writing again. It was important to me that this book would not just be a one-time read but rather, a guide.

I spilled my words on the pages and didn't hold anything back. As the years passed in my lifetime I noticed that many of my old ways didn't serve me anymore. I had to do some major re-setting. Therefore, in this book you'll find my personal references of hardships, struggles, abuse, happiness, gratitude and fulfillment. A life that might be similar to others reading the pages. We all have a story, don't we?

So let's live the rest of our lives to the fullest. Let's make them our greatest days and throw a whole lot of awesomeness into the mix!

Heather

CHAPTER ONE

Re-Discover your YOUTHFUL SPIRIT

RE-DISCOVER YOUR YOUTHFUL SPIRIT

Tip#1   Go out and PLAY

Our Moms were right. We've got to get outside and *play!*

Somehow, for many of us, the walls closed in. As we conformed to the rules of our jobs, society and what is expected of someone over 50, we lost something.

Life became a routine. Many of us did what was expected of us and, amongst other things, we got so busy making our exit plans we forgot about our living plans.

I suggest that it's time to focus on fun again! Somehow, many of us have forgotten how to play. If you can relate, you are not alone. Embrace the next forty or so years with a new, revitalized view. It's time to feel youthful again! Why not find that child inside you who wants to kick off your shoes, run through the grass, fly a kite or chase the dog around the house?

When we were kids there was no social media. The T.V. only had a few channels and our imaginations dreamed up exciting things to do. Some of us just played in the backyard by ourselves, skipping rope or practicing our track and field jumps, while others got friends together and played tag or hide-and-go-seek. There was always some form of play to enjoy because it was our routine. We looked forward to it daily.

    I also remember how each evening, playtime would end. Usually, for most of us, it was when the streetlights came on. I would sadly look up and know that my play-day was over. Now that you're older, you can stay out until the stars start to shine! Something we all wished for when we were kids. Why then, do most of us just stay inside and treat each day as if it's not that special? Why don't we add just a little bit of play? I suggest we take the time and perhaps entire days to get some fresh air, stay out late, enjoy our friends and have some fun.

RE-DISCOVER YOUR YOUTHFUL SPIRIT

It's time to remember that for most of us, our Moms were right. We need to play more.

How could you start playing again?

Name 3 things you could do to get your child-like spirit back...

1. _____

2. _____

3. _____

Tip #2   Make up a FUN LIST

One way to start bring a sense of *play* back into your days is with a FUN LIST.

    I remember, years ago, how I decided to do something creative with my vacation and fun goals. I took four sheets of 8 x 10 paper and titled them: Winter, Spring, Summer and Fall. I then set a yearly budget for FUN things and filled in everything I wanted to do over the next 365 days.

    If I knew a favorite band or singer was coming to town, I would write that down with the performance date and beside it put an approximate cost for the two tickets, a light dinner, plus the concert T-shirt (I always seem to buy one of those). I also wrote down our big vacation plans, plus a few weekend jaunts. I also remembered things that I always wanted to do the year before but never got around to, such as a spa day, going to see a musical, the ballet or a special art exhibit.

Then, I slowed my pen down and started thinking about all those things that I loved to do, but cost little-to-nothing. I wrote down a day of hiking, a potluck dinner for my friends (including those I hadn't seen in years). I then thought about my nearest and dearest friends and when and where I could see them. Since my three closest friends live many miles away, it's not convenient for us to see each other on a regular basis, but when we do, it's magical! It's like no time has passed and we're just happy souls sharing stories and laughing out loud. I have a saying that, "we only have so many summers left." It's so important, especially now, to block off time to see them.

There are other things that I love to do such as bike riding along the waterfront trails, playing a board game with the kids, or a game of cribbage. Believe it or not, even cribbage games go on the list. The cost of these is zero so having fun doesn't have to add costs to a budget.

After my list is completed, the cost of each posting item is written down beside the action. At the end of my exercise I add everything up. If I'm over budget, I'm crossing a few things off... but if I'm under-budget that's where I get creative with adding a few more fun ideas!

Time is one thing we can't get back, we must make the most out of this FUN List and cherish our days and weeks for enjoyment.

What could go on your FUN List? Take the time to write just 8 things that you could put on your list. Then grab some colorful 8 x 10 paper and label the seasons. You don't have to start at the beginning of the year, you can start anytime. After all, this could be the most fulfilling To-Do List you write this month!

Things you can put on your FUN List...

Winter	Spring
Summer	Fall

Tip #3   Have something to LOOK FORWARD TO

Having something to look forward to helps keep us energized and youthful.

Let's imagine you're working on your *fun* list and realize that musical play or concert you wanted to go to isn't for another ten months. Wait... don't *NOT* put it on your list! I've booked many tickets for these types of events. You book your tickets, well in advance to secure your seats even though the performance date is a long way off. You may even have to add these events onto next year's *fun* list. Fortunately, for most of us, time flies by and before you know it you will be giddy with anticipation when the special event is only a few days away.

When I book a play or concert I envision the view from our seats. I find videos online that feature songs and I start humming the songs over and over again. I place the ticket confirmation in a place I can see it every day and I've usually got a few months of anticipation to keep the excitement vibe up.

There are a lot of other things you can look forward to (such as a big vacation) but there are smaller things too. Maybe you're like us and all your kids are adults and live many miles away. Plan some one-on-one time with your kids for the next time they come home for a visit. Book those tickets to see their favorite sports team or plan a day at the spa. There are other things too that don't cost a lot of money such as getting the old bikes tuned up and scouting out the local trails.

And... there are probably lots of future events that you don't know about. Check the local paper or community websites. Who knows, you might even find yourself interested in a local charity event that you love being a part of year after year. If you have a significant other, why not plan date nights once a week? They could involve a movie, dinner or even a few hours at a local coffee shop. My husband

and I try not to let a Friday night go by without it being our special date-night.

Haven't you found that even over fifty, the to-do lists and mundane schedules of daily life creep into all months of the year? If you let it be, before you know it another boring 365 days have passed by. I know that for many of us, myself included, those days involve contributing to the care of an elderly parent or fulfilling other obligations that desperately need attention. Why not get in the habit of booking an exciting event no matter how far away it is? Also, grab that community newspaper and find something *fun* to do *this* week. Then, take a moment to notice how excited you feel just because you've got something you're looking forward to!

RE-DISCOVER YOUR YOUTHFUL SPIRIT

List two performances, concerts or plays you always wanted to see and write them down. Later, check out their website and see when they're coming within driving distance to your area...

1. _____

2. _____

Think about local events you might be interested in. Later check out your local neighborhood website or newspaper for availability or other ideas...

1. _____

2. _____

Tip #4   LEARN New Things

Although they say you can't teach an old dog new tricks, just remember, we're not canines!

Are some of your favorite shows and movies biographies and documentaries? Personally, I love finding out how people got out of their comfort zone and discovered or re-created their own destiny. Most of the time, along their journey, they needed to learn something *new*.

Although the days of being a famous gymnast or Olympian may be over, there are other sporting events that we could master. Take for instance, Pickle Ball. Have you heard of it? This seems to be a popular sport these days amongst the over fifties. There's also tennis, biking and yes, golf! Although I'm not a great golfer, I remember my husband taking me to the golf range and teaching me the right grip and follow-through. He taught me how to putt and etiquette on the greens. I was terrified the first time he took me to a nine-hole golf course. What if I continually miss the ball as I teed off? What if I make big divots in the grass? What if I hit an amazing long shot and hit someone in the head? These were all real worries and concerns. But my patient husband assured me that it was a beautiful day and that it was going to be enjoyable. Most of all, since I had learned the basics, I was ready. I actually made par on one of the holes that day. The sun was shining, there was freshness in the air and I loved driving the golf cart. I see why men and women love this pastime but I can also see how my fear would have been in the way if I hadn't learned some of the basics.

    Another thing that I've found I have a knack and a love for, is technology. I grew up having to change from vinyl records, to 8-tracks, to cassettes, CDs, and now streaming. Sure, I get frustrated when I have 200 (or more like 1,000) unopened emails from companies that are clearly spamming me. Or, when I have a deadline and the WiFi in my neighbourhood goes out. But those inconveniences are small compared to the gains I've made by learning some of the great achievements in technology.

Besides email, streaming music and on-demand T.V., I have a business with Awesome Over 50 that relies mostly on the advances of technology. I have two YouTube channels, a website, and a Facebook business page. I also upload everyday on Instagram. Yes, Instagram! I used to look at my kids scrolling on this social media platform and think, "I'll *never* go on that." But now, I use it in moderation and have found some really cool people that I learn from and share stories with every day. We're inspiring each other to look at things as pro-age and not anti-age. We all get a boost from the positive inspiration.

What else could you learn? Are you planning on re-setting your lifestyle for the future? Fortunately, these days, almost everything has how-to videos available on the internet. I'm looking forward to learning Tai Chi and Yoga. I'd like to learn to be a better cook, study wine regions and, look at me now - I'm learning how to publish a book!

Whatever I learn, I either love it, hate it or I'm somewhere in-between. The most important thing is that we keep our minds and bodies active and energized with the practice of learning something. Studies show that a learning activity creates increased endorphins, cell activity, and strengthens neurological pathways. Doesn't that sound good?

As humans, it's good to get into the learning habit and *yes*, you can "teach us old folks new tricks!"

Name 3 things you could start to learn.

Ideas could include taking art classes, learning to play piano, new language, becoming a better home chef or wine connoisseur. Don't forget technology. Maybe there's a new app or social platform or streaming system you could learn and talk to family, business associates or friends visually more often...

1. _____

2. _____

3. _____

Tip #5   Sometimes LAUGHTER IS THE BEST MEDICINE

Do you remember when you were a kid how most everything was funny? Did you get in trouble at the dinner table laughing at something your siblings did? Why is it that these days most of us have become so serious?

Several years ago I decided to do something about this lack-of-laughing syndrome. Starting with the news. I no longer watch the eleven o'clock news. I haven't for years. Do I still have an idea of what is going on in the world? Yes, of course! Social media is everywhere and I can't even check my emails without knowing what doom-and-gloom message is the flavor of the day.

Would you like to have more *laughter* in your life? Here are a few things I've found that help me laugh (and even have more belly laughs, those are the best kind, aren't they?)

These days I make sure to laugh before I sleep. I'd rather watch a comedy sitcom or a late-night talk show with a funny monologue than try to go to sleep with anxiety and dread.

I'm also carefully choosing who I'm socializing with. Those who gossip or spread negative information about someone are limited in my social circles. I don't have a water cooler, gossip-girls kind of life. I would rather hang out with people talking about funny and positive things than the stories and snickers of gossip.

I spend most of my days with a husband who makes me laugh and a little dog that's forever putting a smile on my face. Pets are a great form of laughter. Take a video of some of the crazy things your pet does and keep a video of them on your phone for when you need a chuckle.

We also have a stack of comedy DVD's at home that we can put on anytime. Of course, we also go outside and *play*!

I've learned that when you laugh, you release good brain chemicals which also could relieve pain and release health-building endorphins. Many believe that this contributes to a healthier, longer life. There are feel-good hormones that promote social bonds. Think about the last time you were in a group and sharing in a good laugh. You wanted to be there. There's a good feeling of togetherness and well-being.

Our life path is a choice. Sometimes we're stuck in a rut of watching the eleven o'clock news because that's what we've always done. Sometimes we hang out with the doom-and-gloomers and listen to gossip because we don't want to miss out on the next big thing to be afraid of. Sometimes we don't go out and play because well, with all the bad news, it's scary out there!

It's time we chose *LAUGHTER*.

If the end-of-days come, I want to be watching a funny movie. Living in fear and dread doesn't seem healthy as we go about our regular lives. I choose laughter and smiles. Who knows, as I mentioned earlier, we might even live longer with all the good hormones flowing through our bodies. Perhaps if we keep laughing a little more we may be blowing out the candles on our 100th birthday. You'll know who we are because we'll have a big smile on our face!

Name 2 ways you could add a little more laughter into your days (and nights)…

1. _____

2. _____

Tip #6   THINK YOU'RE YOUTHFUL… then you are!

Who else is feeling a little more youthful already? Although this is a good start, what else could you do to feel even more youthful?

One way may be to get a little more with the times? Here's a story of how I got there…

When my kids were teenagers and riding in the car they would turn off my rock songs and change the station. I couldn't believe how they could enjoy modern music over my rock-and-roll bands. Rather than start a back-and-forth battle of changing the music, I decided to become a captive audience. The truth is, both forms of music had something to offer. Eventually, I was listening to modern pop and rap on a regular basis. Then, I began to enjoy the lyrics. Words of struggle and overcoming adversity became anthems for not just them, but for me as well. Now, it seems I'm enjoying it all (including my rock-and-roll), but only because I didn't change the station and stay in my comfort zone.

Music is just one way to feel a little more youthful. If you have kids, just listen and watch what they're doing. I'm always curious about a new app or streaming service. That's how I became a YouTuber and on Instagram!

Younger people have an excitement that is very contagious. We still get calls from our kids to see a new movie. We might not have heard of the film, but it's always a fun night out, sharing popcorn at the cinema. I now bond with one of my daughters over thriller movies. It's a genre I thought I could never enjoy but with her, it's fun!

I think feeling youthful is being open again to new experiences even if at first, they don't sound that great. If you find yourself immediately saying "I'm too old for that" or

RE-DISCOVER YOUR YOUTHFUL SPIRIT

"that's not for me." Maybe give it a little more thought, give it a chance.

I remember a while ago when my daughter and I were at a department store and she knocked on the fitting room door with six interesting clothing pieces. Shortly thereafter I was trying on a shocking pink blouse, a lovely moss-green military style jacket and comfy sweaters. I glanced at the mirror and started to feel energized and stylish. If you've been wearing mostly black outfits that may even be oversized for you, it might be time to brighten up your look. Besides feeling more youthful and fashionable it can also uplift your spirits. Once you wear that new look and hear someone say, "you look amazing in that," it will change your energy level. You will feel amazing and you will no longer settle for dowdy and boring.

There are so many other new-fangled things to enjoy, even without the kids. Check out social media and the PRO-AGE and OVER 50 spokespeople for great new ideas that are waiting for you.

Don't forget that anything that involves a little exercise is also a great idea. Maybe an exercise wrist monitor that shows fireworks on it when you reach 10,000 steps or a popular new sport, like Pickle Ball!

I know I've left out lots of ways to feel more youthful. What are some ways that you can achieve this energized new state?

Just name two for now….

1. _____

2. _____

CHAPTER TWO

FOCUS ON A LIVING PLAN not an Exit Plan

FOCUS ON A LIVING PLAN

Tip #7 Re-Tirement or RE-HIREMENT

So you've started to feel more youthful but are you still stuck in a rut in other areas of your life? Are you headed there?

I spoke earlier about focusing on a living plan over an exit plan but society and the advertisers seem to paint a picture that focuses on retirement in our early fifties. Can you see yourself not working at all, even as a volunteer for another forty or so years? This tip is where I would like to plant the seed for the possibility of RE-HIREMENT when you're officially in retirement.

Golf may not be the only thing you want to work at. For many over 50s, either your retirement day is already here or soon-to-be. Maybe you've been offered an early buy-out at your job. Perhaps you feel that you're no longer fitting into your office scene anymore and want to exit. Whatever the reason, retirement after your current job doesn't have to be the only path to take. How can you continue to fill your days with something you love?

Now, if you're thinking about starting a new business, that's great. You might want to check out Chapter 8 of this book for information on how to begin a life of self-employment. But if this option isn't for you, what are you going to do? Well, get out there and re-discover your passions! Most of us still have them. They could be classical music, cooking, wineries, the arts, or caring for pets.

For example, if your passion is helping animals, then maybe you could volunteer your services or work part-time at a local shelter. Maybe you could help out at a doggy daycare or a local dog walking service.

If its music you love, perhaps you can work part-time as an usher at the concert hall. Depending on the venues, you might get to see your favorite symphony, band or singers perform for free.

FOCUS ON A LIVING PLAN

Even if part-time work can't offer you the full security that you had at your old job it still could fill your days with something you love, plus add a few dollars to your bank account and your pension. Do you see how this is working? It's not just about thirty-five years of prior service, the gold watch and then spend the rest of your day's binge watching TV, traveling and playing golf. Use the spare time you have now and into the future to honor your next calling. This time, choose something that aligns with the things you really love.

Choose to believe that fifty-five or sixty-five is not a cut-off date. It is an elder age where the wisdom and compassion you have is respected and can be utilized.

List 2 things you love to do and where you might be able to find Re-Hirement now or in near future:

1. I love to _____

Re-Hirement or Volunteering Options:

_____

_____

2. I love to _____

Re-Hirement or Volunteering Options:

_____

_____

Tip #8 Ignore the OLD-PERSON LABELS

Now we're feeling youthful and getting our passions back. Woo Hoo! Then just as you're making headway, you introduce yourself to someone and describe yourself as *retired* or a *pensioner*. Maybe you want to re-think these labels.

I think it's awesome to rock old age. However, society might listen to your label and think, "that person is old!" There are many other words and descriptions for us old folks, but I don't want anybody thinking we should put out to pasture just yet.

I personally don't like the words *senior*, *retired* or *pensioner*. The stereotypes can lead to discrimination. I'm talking about a segment of society that may deem us unfit for certain things in life. It can also be dangerous when we start to believe the stereotypes that accompany these labels. I say ditch 'em. We're too youthful for that!

It's difficult enough to feel youthful when many life insurance policies won't accept you anymore. If they do they may have a hefty renewal increase if you're a senior. Many mortgage insurance plans also halt at a pensioner's age. The world seems to be writing you off, so you slowly adjust to society's norms. Eventually you're changing your mindset and going out for dinner at 4:30 p.m. to get the early bird special. You look around and see all the grey hairs around you and, even though some people are ninety, you feel this is where you belong.

When you reach retirement, re-think your answer to "What do you do?" Of course, if you want to say you're retired or a pensioner that's OK. But what about, I'm an aspiring horticulturist!" (you love gardening) or "I'm rescuing animals" (you work at a dog shelter). My personal favorite is still, "I've ditched the 9 to 5 and working on my next big adventure." Say your answer with a smile or even a chuckle.

FOCUS ON A LIVING PLAN

After all, you probably have forty plus years left of adventures plus a whole past lifetime of exciting events. Working on your next big adventure may not be a stretch.

The point is, you want to stay engaged in the conversation of life. So, change the label! *YOU* define this chapter of your life.

What's your new introduction story? You have 15 seconds to tell someone about *YOU* without the old-folks labels...

_____

_____

_____

_____

Tip #9   Start YOUR VISION BOARD

So, maybe you're now thinking about your next big adventure from the last tip but you may be stuck on what that will look like and what you could do to get things rolling. Here's a suggestion on how to get started. Have you ever made a vision board?

I believe they actually work and here's my personal recollection on why…

In the 1970s, I drew a picture of what my living room was going to look like in my future dream home. I drew everything in detail from the dark oak floors to the cathedral ceilings, plus a large stone fireplace. Although this drawing wasn't a vision board, it functioned as the same thing. I looked it almost every day. I knew my dream home was on a lake, but having traveled my city's waterfront, I knew I wasn't going to find this home nearby.

FOCUS ON A LIVING PLAN

I'll never forget the day, out of the blue, I said to my late husband, "let's go for a drive." I remembered a small lake about forty minutes out of the city and I just had to get there. We got lost and ended up on some rural route. Then, the other side of the lake appeared. I had no idea this part of the lake even existed! As we drove down a dirt road, there it was - a *For Sale* sign. I had to get inside. I didn't even stop to think. My husband probably didn't even bring the car to a full stop before I jumped out. The owner was working on her garden and invited us in. It was *THE* house! The stone fireplace, the cathedral ceilings and a beautiful setting right on the lake. Within a few hours, we had drawn up the paperwork for an offer and it was ours!

Do I believe in visions and vision boards? I sure do! If you think that's all a bunch of hooey I'm here to tell you that I believe that *thoughts* can become *things*. These days, my husband and I do up a vision board every year. We include things that are easy to achieve such as trips and electronics. But then there are the dreams, the visions of things we have not yet accomplished. Like this book for example. I truly want it to reach a large amount of people. I want many of the over 50s to dream again and envision a wonderful, fulfilling and awesome life.

What does your future look like? How about going to the dollar store and purchasing bristol board, like you did as a kid. Nowadays, if you don't have many magazines lying around, search the internet, find photos of your hopes and desires, and print them off. You can start a vision board anytime.

There's also a word that's going around these days, 'Manifesting'. I truly believe that's what happened when I found that house. I had drawn it several years before I actually found it. That's another thing, don't be disappointed if your biggest dream doesn't come true right away. Some of the smaller ones will. Just re-paste the unanswered vision onto your newest

FOCUS ON A LIVING PLAN

vision board and expect that if it's meant to be it will soon show itself.

Some of the material things that I used to think were important on the vision board no longer matter. I don't need a mansion anymore. I've downsized and frankly, I now believe less is more. I'm still going for comfy furniture and an updated kitchen, but have no need for six bedrooms and six baths.

In addition to the big dreams, put photos of things such as a photo of an over 50 person riding a bike on a trail. Maybe even a bunch of vegetables and a blender. Sometimes, the best way to improve your life is by looking at broccoli photos in amongst the ski trip to the Alps. This will remind you that you need a healthy body to achieve some of those dreams.

It's amazing how visual messages can bring forth reality. So put some ink in the printer, dig up the old magazines, get some white glue and purchase that bristol board.

What could you bring into reality? Make your visions vivid and get excited about your awesome future!

List 4 things you could put on your Vision Board

1. _____

2. _____

3. _____

4. _____

Tip#10   Don't look back ...
It could be A TRAP

I talk about using past experiences as examples, but I like to look and live in the *here* and *now* or glancing at the *future*. If I had a choice, being in the present is the best place to be. Looking towards the future can be a pretty close second as long as you have your rose-colored glasses on.

    The reason that looking back is a trap is that no matter which way you look at your past that former person doesn't exist anymore. The past also seems to harbor and bring out negative old patterns, like guilt and regret. Even if we look at the bright side of the past, it could still be a trap, especially if we believe that life was so much better in the *good old days*. The past can trick us into thinking that growing old will never amount to that kind of an amazing life. This is a huge trap that will swallow you up. Why is it that we don't remember the hardships and pit-falls? Remember how we needed to excel in school, find a career, find a partner and adjust to social pressures to fit in? Your memories of how great you looked in a swimsuit doesn't compare to the confusion and angst you felt back then. So I suggest you live in the present with a few amazing dreams about your future.

As I mentioned, dreaming about the future is a pretty close second to living in the present. Just make sure it swings to the side of hope, and not worry. We will talk in Chapter Eight about big dreams, but don't forget about the little ones too.

I'd like to share a story about how everyday living can give you excitement about your future and you could enjoy each precious moment in the *here* and *now*…

My youngest daughter and I planned a wonderful day together, where we knew the restaurant we would go to, evening stop at a fancy coffee shop and yes, shopping. I had decided to take her to the most fashionable shopping center in our city.

    We started our experiences at her suggestion, a new Japanese restaurant with a conveyor belt that brought food to our table. The restaurant also had a clever electronic tablet ordering system. (I thought I was in a futuristic movie). The sushi and other items we ordered were amazing in presentation, and delicious! We took our time savoring each dish and ordered slowly, enjoying each moment.

    After dinner we did some mother-daughter browsing through book stores, fashion boutiques and home décor shops. Later, as planned, we went to the fancy coffee shop and I had tea with silver tea service and my daughter had a chai latte. We took our time and shared baguettes and cheese with a strawberry preserve. We were surrounded by lush green plants and chandeliers overhead. It was as if we were transported to a European city. We had both dreamed a small dream and it came true. We cherished the special moments together and sipped our hot drinks until the mall closed. We spent our planned day together and made it a reality savoring each event.

One day, we'll plan another mother and daughter day. It will be something entirely different. I'll look back at this past experience with a smile, but only as a glimpse. I'll look forward to something new to experience with her.

The wonder of something to look forward to is the dream, but the fun and magic is in actually enjoying and savoring the moments in the *present.*

There's an old saying, "don't look back unless you want to live there." Truly, there's nothing there but some old memories. It's time we look ahead of us and take this moment to look around. Who or what is in front of us right now. Let's enhance our moments and take the time to give them our full attention.

There are other questions that come up for many of us as we think about spending precious moments with our loved ones. Who are we taking for granted? How could we put a little more together-time into our days? This goes for planning time with best friends as well as family members. Even the dog could maybe get a little more attention and a bit more play time.

Time has a habit of floating away quickly, especially as you get older. The future for you should have its rose-colored glasses on but be aware as you step into the precious moments of the *present*. Remember to take each moment as it comes and enjoy and feel it fully as it unfolds. After all, that's where the real magic is going to happen.

Tip #11   Frappuccinos, Tapas & Sushi, OH MY!

Life is a banquet and why not have a taste of most everything? Although this saying relates metaphorically to everything in life I think it's time for many to get away from the same old food. This includes the way it's served. Whether you dine out or make something new at home, food can also be delicious for all of your senses.

    To give you an example of trying new foods, I'd like to elaborate on the Japanese restaurant experience that I mentioned in the last tip…

    I described how we ordered food from an electronic tablet and the food arrived at our table by conveyor belt. What an experience! Now, although I love sushi, this restaurant had other dishes that I had never heard of. The ordering process was complicated, as you swiped left and right on the electronic tablet screen to find all the selections on the menu. The photos looked appetizing but there were only three word descriptions. Also, most of the fish and other menu items I had never tried before. One of the good things about dining with one of your kids is that you can say "you pick the selections tonight," and let them control the tablet and ordering.

     We decided to start with two miso soups (yay, something I knew)! In less than three minutes, the conveyor belt brought us the soup. I panicked as I grabbed my soup off the conveyor belt. I didn't want it to be whisked away and disappear into the abyss of conveyor belt-land. I'd be too embarrassed to 'ding' my server (there's a place on the tablet to click for your server) and tell him my miso soup was missing and lost in the restaurant somewhere. As we sat there watching other people's dining selections fly by us, I realized that this was fun! My wide-eyed daughter couldn't wait to tap the menu for the next creation. I could definitely chalk this up to a great experience. Now, I must admit, some of the dishes I tasted, I passed on. Not everything is going to be to your tastes, but would I miss the experience? Not on your life!

How do you feel about sushi? I went to an authentic sushi bar in the 1980s. It was part of an after-party for a movie I had a role in. It was the real deal of raw fish and I had mixed feelings about it. I slowly learned that California rolls with ginger were great ways to start myself on these delicacies. Now, I'm into raw fish in every way including in an ice cream cone style.

These days, I'll try most foods. Even the exotic, hot and spicy ones. Some of my new favorites are calamari (squid) and almost anything with guacamole. I'm excited to try a new hot sauce and dine in a restaurant with foods and a culture I've never experienced before.

I also love to try new wines and cocktails in restaurants. Recently, I tried a Moscow Mule and a Manhattan. I never tried them before and now these are my new favorite drinks. I even like the fact that many restaurants serve these drinks with one single huge ice cube, usually in a sphere shape.

I also get excited when I visit my local coffee shop and see their new creations. I've learned that I love chai lattes but I'll never again order a pumpkin spiced coffee. You take the good with the bad, depending on your taste buds, but it is still inspiring.

Many of my restaurant food experiences, such as tapas, get me into tastes and foods that are new to me. They can also give me a taste of culture. Like a Greek restaurant when the server lights up a dish of cheese with a huge flame and the patrons in the restaurant shout, "opa!"

You can also bring the tastes and serving suggestions home (without the conveyor belt). As for coffee, there are many coffee machines that you can buy for home. Why not enjoy the coffee house feeling in you pajamas. Frappuccinos, lattes and espressos, oh my!

    If I'm making or ordering-in sushi I'll have the special bowls and spoons at home for miso soup. I'll have chopsticks as well (with a fork on the side for guests) For Mexican meals, I'll have guacamole bowls and put out a few different bottles of hot sauce (including the extra-spicy green ones)! At home, I also have the copper mugs and the sphere ice cube trays so I can share and enjoy delicious Moscow Mules.

    Food and drinks are for the senses to enjoy. Back in the day, I would just order a rum and coke as my choice of cocktail. My dining choices were mostly steak houses. Now, I go to specialty lounges that offer six different types of Manhattans and I make reservations at restaurants I've never been to.

FOCUS ON A LIVING PLAN

As I said earlier, "life is a banquet, go out and taste as much as you can!" I want to travel the world and experience many cultures. But, in the meantime, I'm satisfied staying in my local area or at home with my cookbooks, experiencing and tasting the spices and foods that make these countries so amazing. I want to taste it all in this banquet of life…just don't give me another electronic tablet to order from just yet… I'm still working on that!

CHAPTER THREE

RE-JUVENATE & RE-CHARGE

Tip# 12   Be a MOVER

"If you want to stay youthful, you have to keep moving." There's another saying that states, "sitting is the new smoking" and I think most of us can relate.

Although many of you may have work-out rooms, private gym memberships or personal trainers, I'll be talking about a simpler plan. Easy steps that can become long term healthy habits. Gentle exercises that are achievable to most.

Now, for some of you, any kind of exercising might be hazardous to your health. I suggest you have a check-up and find out what you can and cannot do. Yes, we hear of ninety-year old people who run marathons or lift weights but they were fit, monitored and had professionals to help them.

How about, we have a *get-moving mindset?* This will help you achieve many of your things on your bucket list and keep you youthful.

Here's a short story to emphasize a *get-moving mindset…*

My husband and I were making plans to sell our home in the suburbs and move to the city. I had played a lot of competitive tennis as a kid and I was happy living in a home without many stairs. The problem was, the neighborhood in the city that we wanted to move to did not have any bungalows. I had convinced myself that my knees were a disaster from all that starting and stopping in tennis. I was sure I needed therapy or surgery. I was fifty-eight years old and could see walking with a cane in the not-so-distant future. In the city, we fell in love with a two-storey home with fourteen steps up to the second floor. Bill is an athlete (he has always played hockey and goes out for regular bike rides). We moved into the home and he suggested I take the stairs as much as possible. He felt that the constant workout would strengthen my knees. I had no choice but to give this a try. Now, nearly six years later, there is isn't a peep out of me about my knees. I was babying them and they were probably rusting out. I just needed to get them moving.

    Besides the stairs, I also put on upbeat music when I'm making dinner and dance like no one is watching. Sometimes I'll dance around for forty minutes while waiting for the oven to cook a dish. That's a good workout. I still can do a few high kicks and *the twist* to move all parts of my body.

    My husband Bill has also encouraged me to ride a bike. You can rent bikes in most cities and towns but if you have your own bike, you might be more inclined to explore more trails and bike paths. Just remember to keep your bike tuned-up and don't forget safety. Purchase a helmet, lights, and a bell. I ask my speedster husband to take it slow when we're bike riding together. I want to drift by the waterfront trail and watch the ducks and boats. I can take a deep breath of fresh air and be one with nature. We also add a coffee shop destination on our ride so that we have a reward for all that exercise.

A while ago, I introduced Bill to wearable exercise monitors. The other day he did over 16,000 steps and 50 flights of stairs! All he did was walk the dog a few times and move cameras and lights up and down the stairs to set up for my make-up video. These monitors really encourage you to walk more and they reward you with virtual badges for accomplishments (perhaps he only brought up one piece of camera equipment at a time so he could be proud of his day)! I also have a stationary bike and have a routine for riding it and lifting five pound weights.

How could you incorporate easy ways to get a *moving-mindset?*

Do you work in a building where you could take the stairs?

Do you have an old bike you could dust off and refurbish? A stationary bike for inclement weather?

Do you have a dog? It could probably enjoy a few more walks.

These are just some of the ways in which we could get into simple exercise routines that aren't difficult to follow. Let's stop rusting out and get moving again!

What are 2 *moving* exercises you could keep up on a regular basis?

1. _____

2. _____

Tip#13   ...and a SHAKER

Why not be a MOVER *and* a SHAKER?

When I say, *Shaker* I'm talking about literally shaking up real foods (such as fruits and vegetables) in a blender.

Although there are many kinds of bottled smoothies, nothing compares to a smoothie freshly made in your kitchen. Now, if buying fresh vegetables or fruits on a semi-daily basis seems like a stretch, don't forget about the frozen veggies and fruits. Most of these are flash-frozen and still maintain their nutrients. Think about strawberries, blueberries, mangos and even kale. You never have to worry about what's in season and the drinks still taste great.

These days I also make soup in my blender. Hot soup with broccoli and cheese or an amazing tomato basil soup can be made in just a few minutes (Disclaimer... not all blenders can make hot soup or blend frozen fruits and vegetables). Don't forget to check that out when you're buying a new blender or you might experience a burning motor.

If you're making these kinds of shakes, you're eating healthier. Most of us never get enough fruit or vegetables in a day. Yet, we know how much vitamin C or antioxidants from berries and green veggies could help us.

Let's re-visit those over-the-counter and store bought smoothie and green drinks. They are a good alternative if you're constantly on-the-go. However, if you set aside a bit of time in the morning to make your healthy drinks in a blender it might work out better for you, especially if you're on a budget. Take a good look at the price tag of those drinks. If you're watching your budget, in the long run, a good blender and frozen fruit and veggies work out better.

Once you get your blender, experiment with different smoothies. My green smoothie consists of frozen kale, an apple, spring water, lime juice and a little maple syrup. Who knew that kale could be so delicious? There's also the reliable strawberries and banana with added orange juice and spring water. I usually add frozen blueberries to get in the extra anti-oxidants.

    Don't forget to check online for recipes or perhaps buy a blender cookbook. There you will probably find other foods to make in your blender such as salsa or frozen fruit gelato!

    I discovered that a strange thing happens when you get in the habit of eating healthy. Over time, for many of us the sugary cookies and fast food don't taste as good anymore. Some of us even lose the sweet tooth. Now, although many fruits such as orange juice have some sugar content, I'd rather have that mixed in a smoothie or on its own than be drinking a huge bottle of soda.

These days, my freezer is stocked all the time with frozen veggies and fruits. They last a long time and are at-the-ready for a quick drink or bowl of soup.

So why not start be a *mover* and a *shaker?* In this chapter of your life, it's a new way to look at an old saying… and a way we can be at the top of our game!

Tip #14   These boots are made for WALKING

Do you remember when you first heard this phrase? It's an oldie, but a goodie. Of course, my connotation is completely different. I touched on walking for exercise in Tip# 12, but let's take a look at a scenario many of us might be able to relate to…

That comfy leather chair you bought for yourself that rocks back and forth and folds into a lounger might be getting too much use these days (I know, I have two of them). The chair beckons you to sit down and relax after dinner. Maybe, later in the evening, a fancy liquor or scotch finishes up the scenario. All we need is a silk robe and a cigar and there's the over-50 lifestyle our parents always dreamed of! If you have fallen into this pattern as I have in the past, I think it's time we get up, get out and get walking.

RE-JUVENATE & RE-CHARGE

Now, if you've been to the gym, walked all the necessary steps for the day and basically kept moving, that's great. You deserve that comfy chair but if not, let's think about going for a walk. Science says it usually takes about 30 days of consistency before a disciplined routine becomes a habit (so long as you repeat it over and over). Walking usually just requires comfortable walking shoes and a safe pathway. If you have ability to do it, why not start tonight?

    Let's take my master-walker husband Bill for an example. Bill walks our dog three times a day, so he has the walking thing covered. If you are thinking about getting a dog, don't just build a dog house or tie the dog in the yard. Walking a dog in the fresh air is a great way to keep moving and keep your dog healthy too. Our dog is now 10 years old and Bill hasn't missed a step.

    Once you get walking as a routine, it becomes a preferred way to travel to many destinations. Wherever we can, Bill and I prefer to walk places than take a cab or drive.

In the past, when we would visit a new travel destination, I would put on my exercise monitor and plan for 15,000 steps a day! Now that Bill has one, I'm sure we'll up it to 20,000!

In 2019, Bill and I realized our long-term dream of going to Paris. Walking from the Louvre through Les Champs-Elysees, stopping at a local café, marvelling at the architecture and gardens, we discovered a feeling of presence and belonging. It's so much better than just zooming by as a tourist on a double-decker bus. We also did the same thing in London. Rome is next on our bucket list and for sure, we'll have our walking shoes on and exercise wrist monitors charged up!

It's so easy to get your steps in, even at home. You don't have to set a high amount, just 5,000 steps is great. I have fourteen stairs in my house from the upper floor down to the main floor. That's twenty-eight steps up and down. In the past, I would wait until I had a bunch of things to do in one descent. But now, the more I check the mail, make tea and pour my water bottle for myself on other levels, the more steps I accumulate.

It's also great to discover the surroundings where you live. Bill and I lived in suburbia and walked many park paths close to our home. Now that we live in the city, we make it a point not to drive to our local bank, the wine store or the pet shop. Even if it's raining, we put on our raincoats and bring an umbrella. As for the Winter, we trudge through the sleet and snow and get those steps in. After-all…our boots are made for *WALKING!*

Name three places you could start walking on a regular basis and when...

1. _____

    when? _____

2. _____

    when? _____

3. _____

    when? _____

Tip #15 You LOOK MARVELOUS!

I remember when this phrase was popular. Although it's no longer the mid 80s with big hair, big shoulders and bright neon colors, many of us still have a little of that fashion sense inside us. The question is, how is your outward fashion sense these days? Many people I have talked to have said that now that they are over 50, they have a dismissive attitude towards it. Perhaps it's time for a little re-charging and rejuvenating with how you appear to yourself and the world.

If you're not sure if I've described *you*, maybe ask yourself a few questions…

Do you seem to wear mostly black? Do you do that because you feel it makes you look slimmer?

Do you think of trends and fashion as something just for the younger people, or for designer followers?

Do you refuse to wear jeans because they are now *too young* for you?

Do you wear over-sized clothes to hide your extra weight?

Have you lost your authentic self in the process? Are you just a shadow of that person you use to be?

Perhaps you can relate to the above and you know you've neglected your own unique style. Fashion can be fun. It connects us with ourselves and our personal expression.

I answered *YES* to those questions a few years ago. I was absolutely stuck-in-a-rut. I wore mostly black, oversized clothes and wondered why I kept gaining weight. Even as a former model, I had conformed to a frumpy style and lost touch with fashion and trends.

RE-JUVENATE & RE-CHARGE

Lately, as I've decided to rock this chapter of my life, I'm wearing a rainbow of colors. I now wear my outfits in the right size (it even helps me to control my weight as the zippers still need to close). I love my jeans and keep an eye on what's trending.

I remember, just a few years ago, I would ignore the animal prints. I thought they might be too flashy for me. Then, one day, I decided to give them a try. I started off slow with just a leopard animal print scarf. Now, I've gone full *animal* with shoes, skirt, tops and even an animal print jacket. I don't wear them all at once, but I feel re-vitalized when I'm wearing each piece, especially my leopard print pencil skirt. Can you hear me *ROAR*?

The truth is, sometimes we feel stuck. We buy the same style of black pants or tops over and over and get discouraged because eventually the stores don't carry our favorite style or fit anymore.

Why not give something new a try and *dump the frump*? Maybe a slender cut stretchy pair of jeans? Try them on and do a little dance in the change-room. Could that possibly be a more vivacious *YOU* staring back? What about the shorter length pants or trousers? Is covering your shoes and boots still the way to go? Or, should you tailor the hem to a new length that's been in fashion for years? (I'm also speaking to the men out there).

What about those bulky, over-sized clothes? As I mentioned earlier, I used to think that bulky, no-shape clothes would hide my extra weight. In fact, my oversized clothes made me look bigger than I was. Now, I find clothes that are actually my size and I look for super stretchy material in fitted dresses, skirts, pants and jeans. I'm a curvy woman now and proud of it!

I may not wear every fashion trend that comes and goes, and I'm not suggesting that for you either, but lately, I've embraced retro looks, fringes, animal prints, polka dots and bright colors. These styles feel much more aligned with who I am and the awesome person I want to be in the coming years.

Get that *YOU*thful buzz back and once again, hear those amazing words ...*You LOOK MARVELOUS!*

What's a fashion style or two that you could try on the next time you're shopping?

1. _____

2. _____

Tip# 16   SELF-CARE is *Not* Self-ish

If you're like me, you've spent much of your life people-pleasing, and doing most of the things that put your personal needs second.

In this chapter of our lives, it's time to step back, step away and practice more self-care. It's time to stop believing that a little TLC and self-love is selfish. If we're not looking after ourselves, we aren't going to have enough steam to help anybody, especially as we get older.

Remember when you've been on a flight and the attendant starts talking about the oxygen masks? They urge parents to put on their masks first before applying them to their children. It makes sense because if you pass out, you're not going to be of any help to your kids. This metaphor is referenced time and again in our daily lives and it continues to be a great one for all of us who are taking care of everyone else before attending to our own needs.

If you've heard of the *Sandwich Generation* many of us are the *'cheese'* smack in the middle of it. As for me, I have four grown children that still need love and support, plus a ninety-five year old mother-in-law and a brother-in-law with special needs where Bill and I are the only family members available to help. Although I love them all, putting others needs before your own can be draining at times.

Our new home in the city is just a two minute drive from Bill's mother and brother. I wanted to make the move because of love. However, there's a silent voice, whether it's my conscience or society, that pushed me to be more attentive to others. Self-care used to take a back seat for days or even weeks. Sometimes, this was more than my mental health could handle. The result was a feeling of being worn out and suffocated. I guess I forgot to put my oxygen mask on first!

We now have two health care workers who provide daily care for Bill's Mom. Fortunately, Bill's brother lives in the same house as his Mom and he can make simple meals for the both of them. They are great company for each other. At ninety-five, Bill's Mom is now immobile except for taking a few steps with a walker. Alzheimer's is starting to intensify. She can verbalize that she doesn't want to leave her home and we don't want to put her through the drama of moving to a nursing home quite yet. We also have to think of Bill's brother. He will always have special needs and requires a lot of love and care from his sibling. It's an ever-evolving situation.

    Bill and I decided decades ago that we should have a date-night once a week. So far, we've tried hard to keep them up. In the past, taking time to care for our marriage involved babysitters as we headed off for a dinner or a movie to recharge our batteries. Today, the kids are grown but there are still times when we both need to rejuvenate. Besides our date night, Bill plays hockey with his old high school friends and I take *'me'* time as much as possible. Almost every night, I retreat upstairs, take a long bath and spend a little time just relaxing. The demands from others in my life has not eased up since I've entered this chapter of my life. I do know however, that stress is a killer. If I don't look after myself, I won't be any good to anyone.

      The airlines are right. It's time for us to look around at the chaos that sometimes surrounds us and look up. Pull the self-care towards you and breathe in for rejuvenated energy. You deserve it.

Name 3 ways you can introduce a little more *Self-Care* into your days...

1. _____

2. _____

3. _____

Tip #17   One or Two-Day GET-AWAYS

Sometimes, some of the best laid plans for a trip around the world fade away. The dog pines at doggy daycare. We find ourselves the caregiver of an elderly parent. There could also be surprises, such as a leaky basement that take most of our travel fund to fix.

We make excuses and many of them are valid, but why do we postpone even a couple of days as a get-away for well-needed rest and relaxation until another year, or not at all?

Bill and I fell into that trap. Earlier on, it was understandable that we didn't want to take vacations together and leave four young kids at home with sitters, but even after the kids were older, we still found ourselves making excuses why we couldn't travel.

These days, we've re-evaluated and usually book a big trip once a year. Although we plan the trip in detail, the date is usually confirmed at the last minute and we only travel for a week, max. We may pay a little extra for the flight and may not get into the hotel of our choosing but we can live with these concessions. We need to know that Bill's Mom is in good health and cared for and that our daughter is available to babysit our little Yorkshire Terrier. This one-week big trip is great but most of us need more than one week a year for a change in scenery and relaxation. That's why day trips or two day get-aways are important.

    Once a year, we usually book a spa retreat on a lake that's only two hours away from our home. It has a five-star restaurant, a tennis court, a spa-pool with massage jets, registered massage therapists and free rentals of canoes and kayaks. The rooms have sliding glass doors that overlook the lake. Each room has its own fireplace and a tub built for two. This resort is situated in a tranquil spot that feels like a little piece of heaven.

I remember one morning... I got up at 6 a.m. and looked out the window. There in the morning mist, was a beautiful deer locking eyes with me, she seemed to say, "Welcome, you deserve this!"

We've gone on these two day trips to the lake for many years now. After our stay, we feel as if we've been away for a week. We've recharged our batteries and rejuvenated our love.

As for one-day trips, you may want to find a great hiking spot, enjoy a bike trail, or go to a small town and take in a festival or event. If you are like me, you'll feel a relaxing sigh as you leave your driveway. The pressures of work and family are left behind you for a few hours.

The main thing is to get lost. Lost in the moments of discovering new things, lost in the tastes of a new dining experience, or lost in just the magical sound of a canoe gliding on the water with the faint sound of a loon in the distance.

The amazing thing about these jaunts is, when we come home, everything is good. Everyone and everything survived us being away and yet *we're* different. We've allowed ourselves to get back to nature, rejuvenate and to listen to our inner soul.

The noise, the needs, and the ambushes of things that get on your nerves can become a cycle. You buy into the fact that no one can live without you so you bypass self-care, slowly another 365 days go by.

If you stop for a moment and take a deep breath, you can put aside the noise of your everyday life. Take the next step that you deserve and plan a get-away. Rest and rejuvenation beckon you.

RE-JUVENATE & RE-CHARGE

Name 3 places you could go for a one or two day trip...

1. _____

2. _____

3. _____

CHAPTER FOUR

Defying BIRTH CERTIFICATE DATES

DEFYING BIRTH CERTIFICATE DATES

**Tip#18   What if there NEVER WAS A
            BIRTH CERTIFICATE?**

What age are you in your mind? Most of us may say an age that's much younger than the one on our birth certificate. Let's call this our *mindset age*.

I'll give you an idea of what I mean with my own example...

Age forty-two seems like a good number for me. At forty-two, I remember exuding self-esteem, youthfulness and a strong sense of myself. I wore my hair long with confidence and the latest fashion styles looked good on me. My birth certificate lists me twenty-three years older than forty-two. I truly disregard that certificate paper and instead focus on my forty-two year old *mindset age*– confident, youthful and strong.

Of course, we need to consider our bones and body strength before we think we're twenty and book a trek to the top of Mount Everest, or enter into a gruelling marathon.

These days, if someone tries to label me a senior or a pensioner, I just laugh it off. As I said in Tip# 8, I don't acknowledge that label and I don't want to wear it.

Decide what *YOUR mindset age* is. Then, take a few minutes and figure out what you liked to do back in those days. There are probably many good memories. What did you do then that you could still do today? Maybe you had get-togethers and laughed out loud at your attempts to sing karaoke. Maybe you loved to canoe or kayak. Perhaps you started to write a book, painted beautiful landscapes or created abstract art. Whatever you loved to do back then might still hold a passion deep inside you. The true *YOU* is there, with your hidden talents and the joy you felt back then.

Real time is a thief when it labels us and defines us in a way that doesn't celebrate our

DEFYING BIRTH CERTIFICATE DATES

true selves. We can't let a couple of numbers on a birth certificate define us today or in our future.

Now, I exude confidence and self-esteem, youthfulness and a strong knowing of myself. I wear my hair long (although it's silver these days) and the latest styles still look good on me. I'm not going to let a birth certificate change that!

Remember your *mindset age*. Take it with you each day and enjoy living it.

Take time to reflect...

What is your *mindset age*? _____

What are two things you enjoyed doing at your mindset age? What can you re-ignite and recapture today?

1. _____

2. _____

Tip#19   It's Your Party...
WEAR WHAT YOU WANT TO!

I touched on fashion and style in Tip#15 (You look Marvelous). Keeping up with a few trends can keep you looking and feeling up-to-date and maybe instill that rejuvenation you're looking for. How does your age affect how you dress these days?

In social media it's common for people to judge and post hateful comments to those who don't conform to what they believe are the norms of our age group.

Since I have chosen long hair, almost every day some well-meaning or perhaps not-so-well-meaning person tells me to see a hair stylist and get a shorter "age-appropriate" haircut. They may not even be a stranger. Sometimes it's a relative or friend. I also wear skinny jeans, knee-high boots and I'm thinking about getting a tattoo. I'm way out-there in terms of the so-called rules of aging, but I think

DEFYING BIRTH CERTIFICATE DATES

that as a woman over 50, I'm old enough to be finally be *ME*!

With respect to my tattoo, I want something with a memory or inspirational message. Well-meaning people have already told me it's a mistake and eventually I'll hate it. They also explain how it hurts to remove it later. What they are really saying is that it's not for them. Humans have a real need to think that their friends are just like them and always will be, but many times we've just grown differently and feel like expanding our horizons.

Perhaps you've decided to get back into makeup. Many of your friends no longer wear makeup, but you just had a makeover at a local mall and feel marvelous. How long before a co-worker or friend says, "so when did you start painting your face?" Perhaps your mother-in-law says, "that lipstick is too red for you!" Do you go home and wash your face? Do you throw $200 worth of makeup in the trash? *YOU* are your own judge and jury. If you can confidently look at yourself in the mirror with your age spots covered, an even color and texture to your face with a great foundation makeup, your eyes sparkling with mascara and a bold lipstick color that makes you feel like a fashionista, then I say, *"go for it!"*

On the other hand, I have some amazing friends and followers who support me. It's okay to have fewer true friends. If friends or social media followers make you feel uncomfortable with their sarcasm and strong opinions, it may be time to seek out the true friends who applaud who you truly are. Maybe it's time to press the *block* setting, both in real life and virtually.

Now I guess I should add a caveat here… be careful, are you actually going through a midlife crisis? If you've chosen a face tattoo or just bought full leather gear for a coast-to-coast summer trip on a motorcycle (that you've never ridden before), your true friends may just be trying to help. It's always good to take a good look and know the difference between growing and retreating or running away from this chapter of your life.

What are a couple of things you could do if you blocked out judgement from others

1. _____

2. _____

Tip# 20   Are you feeling INVISIBLE?

So you've tackled the so-called age rules and are finally feeling like your authentic self again, but somehow the world didn't get the memo. You feel *invisible.* This time, the silver in your hair and those darn wrinkles may be the culprit, but let's not fall into this trap!

According to studies, women in particular feel invisible by age fifty-one. Confidence plummets after age fifty.

Do you remember when you were younger playing super hero games? If you had a choice to have a superpower many of us would choose to become invisible, but this kind of aging *invisibility* is nothing like that. To us over 50s, feeling invisible at times is a weakness. Society, knowing or unknowingly, can't see our worth or acknowledge we're important. I say this because feeling *invisible* has happened to me, and I consider myself a confident person!

Invisibility seems to show up a lot in stores. As you know, I've let my natural grey and silver hair grow out, I don't look like I'm in my thirties or forties anymore.

I remember when I was left standing at a grocery checkout just as it was my turn to pay. The cashier turned, saw a well-dressed business man standing at an unattended lottery counter and immediately walked away from me to help him. Was I *invisible*? Did she not see that I was waiting? After she laughed and giggled, "good luck" to the man in the suit, I politely asked her, "if I was invisible"? I didn't ask this to be impolite. The cashier knew I had waited patiently as an elderly woman ahead of me dumped out her handbag to find change to pay for her groceries. I clearly had frozen foods that were thawing. I wanted to know why my ten minutes of waiting was so less important than the thirty seconds the businessman waited at the lottery booth. The apology the cashier gave was genuine, but I don't blame her. Many times, society sees us older generation as people who have time on their hands. It's a stereotype. I would probably bet that I had a busier afternoon than the businessman did. I would like to make another point about this interaction. The cashier was around my age. The disrespect goes all through the ages!

Another time, I was returning makeup and I knew the store's return policy was good. If you didn't like the product you purchased, once you tried it at home, or if the color turned out to not be right for you, they would do an exchange or give your money back. I had my receipt and I explained that I tried it once and the color for the foundation was definitely not for me. This was an expensive cosmetic and I just wanted to exchange it for more suitable color. The clerk gave me a 1-800 number to call. As I waited on my cell phone for someone to pick-up from the call center, it occurred to me that I had just been given the brush-off. Although this woman was the manager of her section, I decided to go to the store manager and see if my suspicions of being brushed-off as a customer were accurate. The store manager was appalled that I was treated in such a way and was happy to give me my exchange. By the time we went back to the makeup counter the clerk had disappeared. It wasn't my intent to get anyone in trouble, I simply wanted to be seen and heard, get the right shade of make up and be treated as though I was a valued customer.

The point of these two stories (and I have more), is not to stay *invisible.* Be a beautiful Phoenix and rise up! You deserve to be treated as well as anyone else, especially if you're over 50. Remember that your birth certificate age does not matter and it should not matter in society. We need to politely call out those who disrespect us because they *think* we're an older person and not a worthy customer. It also seems that to many people, we're just a person who looks like we have lots of time on our hands. Our time is as valuable as anyone else's and, as a matter of fact, we have less of it than most!

I am now aware when people treat me as if I'm *invisible*. When I notice it, I politely bring it to their attention and I don't let people take advantage of me or my time anymore. I believe if we stand up and rise, the *invisibility* tide could turn.

Protect your self-esteem and your visibility. Let's change those statistics of women (and men) and feel more visible after fifty. There's a pro-age movement out there. Let's remind people to respect their elders!

Tip #21 Your Superpower is your CONFIDENCE

We all have a superpower inside us, whether we're young or old, and that's our *confidence*!

I personally know men and women who are not celebrities but can walk into a room and many eyes are drawn to them. It doesn't matter if they're older. They still have that energy and light that is attractive. I believe we can all have this. Do I feel like I have it? ...Hell *yes*! I have worked on my confidence and self-esteem for years and I'm turning the tide on *invisibility*!

In my childhood, I was an ugly duckling and abused at home. I was bullied at school by my classmates. Because of this, I had low self-confidence and self-worth much of my young life. Even when I was a model, I was bulimic because I never thought I was thin enough. I went into an abusive first marriage because that's the relationship I knew from my parents.

In those days, my confidence was weak, but once I figured that we all have a choice, things started to change. When they say, "people walk all over you" it's because we're so weak we're almost lying down. There came a time in my life when I said, "enough of this!" I read books on being a victim and co-dependent and decided to leave my first abusive marriage. I vowed that if there was to be another man in my life, he had better respect me and be a great Dad who respected my daughters. I was growing with confidence, gaining self-respect and building self-esteem.

As you build your self-confidence and self-worth, it seems that nothing is impossible. I've spoken in front of crowds of people with my wobbly legs and a few frogs in my throat, but I made it through because of my confidence. I started a YouTube channel, when many people said that a beauty and fashion channel would only be successful if I was in my twenties. When you charge up your superpower of *confidence*,

DEFYING BIRTH CERTIFICATE DATES

amazing things start to happen. In two short years my very first beauty video on YouTube hit 1.5 million views!

True confidence has to be genuine. You can't think you're top-dog or better than everyone else and you certainly can't fake it until you make it. Put in the work, have a sense of empathy, be humble and watch yourself glow! Confidence is the most beautiful when you walk into a room beaming and you know that you want to listen, interact and have respect for all. People are attracted to that kind of light. Sometimes I'll stand back and watch people in the room peering around for someone better to talk to while they are already in conversation. Next time you are at a networking event or even a large social event, take a look around the room and you will see what I mean. When you honor the light in yourself, you can honor the light in others. Truly listen to that person who has made their way to stand in front of you and be a beacon of light.

Putting social events aside, the first person you should impress with your confidence is *yourself*! It may mean putting yourself first a little more. Remember the tip in this book (Tip#16) S*elf-care is not selfish*. It may be worth a re-read if you're struggling moving forward with self-confidence.

Think about confidence like a muscle. It could be hard to find under all the materialistic trappings that you thought would provide self-worth. A designer handbag and expensive shoes may impress some people but they are a façade.

Once you find your *confidence* muscle, tone it up put in the work and cultivate the energy to attract people to your vibe. You're certainly not *invisible*, you're glowing, confident, empathetic and an all-round better version of yourself.

Shine on, you amazing awesome one!

CHAPTER FIVE

Un-Stuck THE RUT

Tip #22   Find your AUTHENTIC-SELF

In Tip# 19, I spoke about wearing what we want to. Whether it's long hair or a tattoo, wear something that's authentically *YOU*. This tip talks about something a little broader. The full *authentic-self*. Finding the trueness of your being.

    Let's face it. We're all unique. So why do some of us eventually conform to standards or change our actions because others say we should? How do we get back to where once we belonged? Let's start a journey of truly getting back and finding our *authentic* soul. Start by looking at old photos. Where did you find pure joy? Think back to who you were, what you loved to do, maybe what you stood for. A time where you felt the flow of life. Rediscover that true spirit of yourself. If you can't find the true *YOU* in a particular chapter of your life or if you're not proud of the person that you were, move on. It could be waiting for you in your future. I'll get to that later.

In awakening into my *authentic* self, I found it was a time where I spoke up for myself, had confidence, stood up for women's rights (this was in the early 70s) and spearheaded charitable causes and events. Also, ironically, it opened the world of glamour as it opened my mind to the world of fashion and beauty. My authentic-self was percolating.

As I mentioned, I had a difficult childhood, but for a brief time in high school, I found a wonderful version of myself. I must have grown six inches over the summer holidays between grade eight and high school. My Mom let me wear makeup and stockings for the first time. This is when my self-confidence took a good turn and not just in appearances alone. I began volunteering for after-school events and found myself organizing folk rock concerts and charity drives. My authenticity was blossoming and I was doing things I enjoyed. I wasn't sure who this new person was, but I was having fun and going with the flow.

    I knew what I wanted in those days and spoke up if things just didn't feel right. For me, a perfect example of this was in my Algebra class. It didn't hold my interest and I wanted to leave. My guidance counselor told me I could change immediately to an acceptable class-change which was Chemistry. This felt better. However, my Algebra math teacher was furious about the change. He grilled me in the hall, actually yelling at me that I would never amount to anything. Fortunately for me I was a new woman with self-esteem. He couldn't take away my new high-school confidence and I knew he was wrong. I *would* amount to something!

    Another time, I remember I did an English class presentation and defied tradition. I played the recording of Stairway to Heaven by Led Zeppelin for a song review. Most of the class played it safe and featured ballads that they thought the older teacher would like. I got the highest mark in the class and, I made a lot of new rock and roll friends that day.

This new *ME* kept on with flow and momentum. Magical things began to happen. I remember being picked in a class to have a beauty makeover (and to this day, I still don't know why makeup artists were there for my Man in Society class)? I felt gorgeous after the make-over and *authentically* thought I could be a model. I no longer felt like an ugly duckling and I got picked as one of the sweet-hearts of the year for the yearbook.

Now, please understand, I'm not bragging on my looks here or how great I was. This was a magical change that was happening to me as I blossomed. I was growing into an *authentic* person who knew what she wanted and enjoyed where the change was taking her.

The most amazing moment during this time had nothing to do with my looks. I was chosen as one of three students (out of two thousand), by the Principal as the most likely to succeed. I was the only girl, and the three of us were given interviews to well-paying jobs that we could be employed at right after high school. We didn't even need a college degree. At this point, I knew that this teenage girl was *ME* shining, stepping into authenticity and untouched by society's norms (or so I thought). A little note about those interviews…I turned the job offers down. This was the early 70s and I interviewed *THEM*. It was very clear that I would probably stay in the secretary pool at these companies. They were not interested in grooming a woman to be CEO as they would have for the boys… and *YES* I did ask those questions. I had visions at this time and was becoming ambitious. I started to grow into my *authentic-self* and I knew I had much to offer this world.

Now you might ask, "why did you have self-confidence issues as a model with bulimia and in your first marriage"? I had to leave home at seventeen. I didn't even get a chance to go to the prom. My *authentic-self* and confidence then took a nose-dive. My true self-essence was in those high school years. It lay dormant for a while but I got it back around the time of my *mindset age*.

Is *your authentic-self* laying dormant? Isn't it time to find the true *YOU*? It's a great way to get un-stuck and go forward with more of a sense of passion, purpose and a zest for life

I believe you can find your *authentic-self* at any age! Don't worry if you can't find it in your past. You could be a late-bloomer and looking backwards is not where you'll find it. Here's an example…

Maybe you're one of those people who visits a town or country at an older age in the future and finds the culture and people easy to relate to. There seems to be something that's familiar. You find yourself in the flow and you make plans to pack up and move there. It just feels right...your *authentic-self* is beckoning.

Today, I feel connected to my teenage self. I got my groove back and I'm moving to my own beat. If someone says I can't do something I just remember the conversation with my high school math teacher. My YouTube beauty and fashion channel is a perfect example of that. People said no one would watch a sixty-two year old woman doing beauty vlogs, tutorials and reviews but I proved the nay-sayers wrong. I may have some wrinkles and an older body but my true beauty comes from my heart and soul. It shines through with my confidence and a*uthentic-self*.

By the way, I can truly say that today I have a job I love. I march to my own drummer, I'm my own boss and yes... I'm the CEO!

All of our stories are unique and so are our turning points. For me my high school path led me to a path of a pro-age movement and my own business. Yours could be different. You may have found *yourself* with nature as you paddled in a canoe. Perhaps you found *yourself* helping others at a soup kitchen or teaching children in a classroom. All of us are different and so is our growth and discovery of our true essence.

Embrace your unique story and find your *authentic-self*. There's so much magic in finding the true *you*. Continue to enjoy things that give you confidence and happiness. Unearth and grow your talents, and expand and share your energy and soul with others. The world is waiting.

Can you remember a time where you were in-the-flow and your *authentic-self* was blossoming and shining? Write as much as you can about yourself at that time... (use more paper if necessary)

_____

_____

_____

_____

_____

_____

Tip #23   Keeping up with THE JONESES

If you have true confidence, you don't need to keep buying *things* to impress others. It's a trap that I fell into (many of us who grew up in the 80s did). Some over 50s are still stuck-in-a-rut in a *trying to impress* cycle and spending a lot of their *FUN LIST* money in the process.

If you remember the 1980s, you might remember such sayings as "Greed is Good" and "Keeping up with the Joneses." For myself and my friends, this was a chapter of our lives where mortgages were easy to get, house prices were low and we all seemed to have that one thing that seems difficult for the younger generation these days, disposable income. Even though none of us would admit to being yuppies (young urban professionals), many of us drove nice cars and wore designer clothes. These were the status symbols in those days and a way to prove to the world that you had '*made it.*'

UN-STUCK THE RUT

It's been many decades now since the 80s, but many of my acquaintances have the need to prove that, in the game of life, they're a winner. Now, if you like nice things such like an upgraded car, or if you live in an affluent neighborhood, then that's fine. What I'm talking about here is trying to boost your ego and self-esteem through the materialistic show-offs to others.

There's a sense of freedom when you just don't care what others think. Today, I drive an eight-year old convertible and I love it. I know who I am and I no longer have to prove anything to anyone. I live in a modest home and I'd rather spend my money on a trip or memory event than a designer pair of shoes.

Nowadays, many people do not have the disposable income that they had decades ago. If you're over 50, you may anticipate a forced retirement ahead of you and are keeping yourself on a budget. Some have told me that they are barely getting by. We're all part of society and in the end, we're all equal. It doesn't matter what you accumulated in materialistic items. I've never seen a hurst with a luggage rack.

The sayings of "Greed is Good" and "Keeping up with the Joneses," should be taken out of our lives forever. The world would be such a better place if those sayings were replaced with, "Sharing is Good" and "Care about the Joneses." If we no longer feel we have to keep up with the Joneses, we'll have less stress and anxiety. We'll be living a simpler, and probably more meaningful, life.

I've found that living with the phrase, "Less is More" is freeing. If you haven't tried it, give it a go. I think you'll find it makes life a lot less competitive, more relaxed, and you and The Joneses will certainly get along better.

Tip #24   The DOWNSIZING Dilemma

My husband Bill and I have finally downsized our home and we love it! I hope our story acts as words of encouragement and you at least consider what a move like this could do for you.

Prior to downsizing, our family home felt pretty darn comfortable. We had great memories and history associated with our large home. But then, some new realities became clear. Empty bedrooms as our kids got older, high realty taxes, maintenance costs and utility bills. The home had memories but we knew we could make new memories anywhere and keep the old ones in our hearts.

The decision to downsize wasn't quick and easy, but for us, it was the right move. We sold our five-bedroom home that had three fireplaces, an in-ground pool, hot tub and a sauna. It was on a quiet cul-de-sac with only a few neighbors. The house backed onto a ravine (for all intents and purposes, it was a dream home).

Unfortunately (or fortunately for us), this part of the dream was coming to a close. We wanted more freedom and fun in this new chapter of our lives. We sold the big home in the suburbs and moved to a small townhouse in the city.

Now, this was a personal choice. You may continue to be content where you are, or move to the country, or to a warmer climate. You may even choose to move to a small condo and spend your summers at the cottage. Wherever you go, remember that you carry '*home*' within you.

As for us, we're now official city slickers and loving it! We no longer spend weekends mowing the lawn and cleaning the pool. We can travel more without the fear that we'll come home to a forest in our front yard and green slime in the cement pond.

I must say that before we moved the right style of home required some planning, especially in the city. We still wanted our four grown kids to visit us and have areas where they could sleep over if needed. I also wanted a small patch of grass in the backyard for family BBQs and a place for our little dog to run.

We had a few more guidelines. It had to be less than a ten minute walk to the beach (our home was small but we still needed to dream BIG with this beautiful location). It needed to have at least two car parking and be situated on a quiet street. It also had to be less than fifteen minutes by transit or cab to the downtown area where we could have fun on our Friday date nights. With a little bit of searching (and not settling for less), we found it all!

The home we have now is about a quarter of the size of our old one, but it suits us just fine.

It has three bedrooms. One is the master bedroom, the second is our office and the third transforms from an exercise area into a sleepover space in just a few minutes. The finished basement is now our studio where many of our beauty and fashion videos are filmed.

For Bill and I, we can now look back on the various chapters and phases in our lives. We outgrew the apartments that we shared with roommates in our college days. We left one small home, where the kids shared bedrooms, to a home with more space as they got older. Then finally, we realized it was time to downsize from the dream home where we raised them. For many of us, we didn't think much when it was time to grow. Downsizing is just the opposite, it's an out-growing of sorts.

I can only speak from our experience and how downsizing has changed our lives for the better. I suggest you think about it if you haven't made the move yet. No matter where you are, it may be time to consider how you, in your own way, can step into a simpler life of freedom, access to new experiences, and a fresh outlook during this amazing chapter of your life.

Consider what a downsized home would look like for you. Where would it be? How many rooms? What would be your budget?

_____

_____

_____

_____

_____

_____

_____

Tip #25   Remember to TRUST YOUR INSTINCTS

Talking about instincts is tricky, and I'm by no means an authority on this. Sometimes instincts give us confusing messages, such as, "I need to eat this carton of ice cream to feel better."

The best way to describe what I'm trying to say here can be wrapped up in two examples, highlighting the feeling of dread and highlighting the feeling of going on the right path. Two exact opposites, but so important at this time in our lives.

We all know that feeling when the hairs stand up on the back of our neck and we know we have to walk away from something that either seems too-good-to-be-true or to get out of a situation that we feel could harm us. It's a common instinct and response, and not one that easily leaves us. As older people we are prone to predators, especially those who want our life savings. We hear about the scams on T.V. and swear that we'll never fall for that, but, I myself, have been scammed by people many times in my life. I was a trusting person, but I now know how to dig deep into an investment opportunity, truly listen and trust my instincts!

    I remember a time where a person in our community was pitching a so-called once-in-a-lifetime investment to many in our circle of friends, including Bill and I. When we met him at his office, he took us to the parking lot to show off his new high-end car. He wanted us to tap into our savings and told us how much money we would make in just a month or two. The return on investment was, you guessed it, too good to be true! He knew how to spin his web. As we kept chatting, and as he loosened up and felt more comfortable with us, he let something slip when he said, "I've done a lot of deals and this one might actually work"… "Might actually work?!" What happened to secure investment and solid return? The hair was standing up on the back of my head. One word, *might,* saved us from losing $40k.

Remember your instincts when you are feeling that you don't trust a pitch or a person. The more you listen and learn, the more you'll know your *instincts* were right.

There's the second *instinct* that I wanted to talk about and that's the one where we are led to a path because it *just feels right.* Somehow something is beckoning us and our *authentic self* is all ears!

Now, you should listen if a doctor says bungie jumping or rock climbing on the weekends are not good ideas for your health, but as I said, "if you're taking a leap of faith on something that your instincts and *authentic self* tells you to do" (and it's not hurting yourself or others), I say, "Go for it!"

Trusting gut feelings and following our instincts helps us go through life. Freedom is in the flow of life. Instinct is the fuel that helps it run.

Instincts can be magical. They pop up as new goals and dreams and we're driven towards them. Go ahead and paint landscapes if you're inclined! How about doing something about that feeling that love could find you again? Perhaps a lunch date with a person from a reputable match-making site is feeling like a good idea these days. Maybe you've put off moving from your big home in the suburbs but now you read about downsizing and you're inclined to start looking at houses with a smaller square footage. It's that little nudge that you feel will lead you in the right direction, especially at this time in your life.

I had a gut instinct to write this book. I've never written one before, but I sat down day after day allowing my pen to write whatever it wanted and I just let my thoughts flow. I felt the instinct to keep on writing and I've made it through to this point. My pen is flowing and my gut feeling says, "Keep going Heather, you got this!"

What are 2 new things that your heart is instinctively telling you to try?

1. _____

2. _____

Is there something your instincts are telling you to get out of right now?

_____

Tip#26   Are you still thinking about FOMO (fear of missing out)

So, what is FOMO? In my opinion, it is a reaction to real or subliminal messages that creep into our day-to-day lives. The travel agencies and retirement investment companies have a field-day with this one. You see the ads and believe that if you're not traveling five times a year, are part of an exclusive golf club or have a second home on a beach, you are failing at this game of life.

I'm here to tell you, you're not! We have all been dealt different cards with our lives. All of us have made mistakes and some of the bad times were just thrust upon us. If you're stuck-in-a-rut thinking that the perfect, sugar-coated way of life will or has passed you by, I hope this tip helps.

As we watch the commercials on retirement savings plans they suggest that if you start saving early, you'll be a millionaire by age 50. I admire those who made it through their lives, saved and are now considered rich. For people like myself though, who left an abusive marriage with an alcoholic spouse, had no child support or financial help, and was a single parent of young children, it was difficult to save. I was on my own to pay for childcare, shelter, divorce lawyer, after-school activities and everything else a single mother has to deal with. If you were in a similar position, I want to say it's OK. Let go of any shame and live life the best way you can.

Sometimes your obligations seem ongoing. As I mentioned before, Bill and I still have to help with Bill's Mom who is feisty about staying in her own home. Bill's brother lives with her and requires special needs with his disability. We still get out of the country for a vacation once a year for a few days, and have professional care arranged. However, traveling the world on a regular basis is prohibitive.

For many, there could be other factors such as health concerns that keep you close to home. As we work on our self-esteem, this fear of missing out could be downright dangerous. We read and see that we should be energetic and lively as we enter these after-50 years. I know for many, that's not possible. You may have sports injuries, ailments or other health concerns that make a dream lifestyle impossible. "Live your best life" is the right saying. I also say, "embrace each day and make the most of it."

What could you do with what you've got? Let's rename this new adventure LOBL (living our best life) Perhaps, start that new savings account titled the 'FUN LIST', go for long sight-seeing walks, see more plays, take in weekend jaunts…the list goes on and on. Also, take in the good vibes as you hug your Mom, Dad, dog and your kids. It's OK if your life is spent more with loved ones than taking off on a sailing trip around the world. The only thing you could be missing out on is sea sickness and battening down the hatches during a terrible storm.

Did you used to love to watch the shows about the rich and famous? Although many of them were probably wonderful people, I feel a different viewpoint now when I see that recently a diamond and emerald necklace sold for 27 million dollars! How does FOMO even fit into that scenario? I can't imagine wearing that much money around my neck! The playing field certainly isn't level. We can still dream big but let's be happy with the here and now. Let's live our day to day lives to the fullest no matter what.

    We can all re-program ourselves to live a less FOMO-style life. From wanting the diamond jewelry to, as I said earlier, keeping up with The Joneses.

    If you find yourself feeling like you're missing out ...snap out of it! After-all, you're working on making this a great chapter of your life and you're one of the *Awesome ones*!

Tip#27   Embrace the WARP-SPEED World

I'm talking about *technology* here, folks! If you're like me, you probably have a love-hate relationship with it.

    We all get stuck in the old ways, especially when we try to turn off our computers and it needs to do yet another update. There are other times when apps no longer work because our cell phones are too old, or we can't bring in a T.V. station with our rabbit ears anymore. The truth is, times are changing and they're changing, *fast!*

    The other day, I had tickets to a drive-in movie. My usual way of getting my tickets is with the *print at home* feature. I printed out my receipt but in big writing was a warning that only the QVC code on my phone would work for entry. I knew what a QVC code was and brushed it off. I decided I would look into this an hour before leaving home for the event...big mistake!

As I attempted to get the code, I got stuck in a loop. I tried to log-in with my password and email (which I knew were right) but it kept saying they weren't valid.

We decided to get on the road or we would miss the movie altogether. Fortunately there was a 1-800 number and eventually I was speaking to a real person. I grabbed my husband's phone while the customer care worker walked me through the prompts. Nothing was working. He finally suggested that I go to another site that was related to the drive-in and we finally got the code to appear on my husband's phone. We literally were in the line-up for the drive-in and got the code with just minutes to spare.

These days, it's not a matter of loving or hating technology. As the world turns at warp-speed, if you don't re-adjust you're completely left behind.

There are certainly many social media platforms where many of your friends hang out. There are apps where you can see and speak to loved ones in real time all over the world. There are movies that can be downloaded, and at least four different platforms besides cable to watch on your TV. You can listen to your favorite album by speaking into a gizmo on a table and YES, it's true…big brother is watching!

There are a few ways to learn these new-fangled things. Maybe talk to a kid thirty years younger than yourself and learn more about what's going on. Take a course or hire a social media expert or listen to an app guru. Depending on your goals, you'll want to keep up and learn some new skills *now.*

I'll talk later in another chapter about BIG dreams but technology is usually your first step in getting things up and running. Maybe you've decided you need to build a website. How do you take credit cards and debit cards online for your services? The answers can be found in seconds, you just need to know *HOW* to look. Start with the search engines. There, you can find how-to manuals and videos. I also find that there's always a friend of a friend or kid of a friend that knows how to maneuver a particular tech maze.

    Technology is also great for predicting trends that might make any great new idea, investment or job obsolete. I remember in the 90s hearing how house phones (land lines) with visual monitors would be all-the-rage in the future. Later came the mobile phone with it's built-in camera. We all watched land lines quickly become a thing of the past and those visual monitors became bookends.

    Technology has an adjective attached to it: *disruption*. Is your BIG dream to sell a new invention or service? You'll want to make sure there is a market now and in the future for your next great idea. Going the way of the Dodo bird is happening everywhere with new inventions. Do your research. Know where the market is going and whether or not your great new idea or investment into a stock will soon be on the extinction list.

Every one of us has their own way of doing things, but don't shy away from looking deeper into this technology thing whether it's for business or pleasure. We've come a long way from phone books, in-mall surveys and long distance phone calls on our land lines. Isn't it time to get those fingers typing on the search engines and warp-speed to the future where everyone else is already waiting for you?

What's a new technology, app or social media platform you have been meaning to learn about? Think of 2 of them ...

1. _____

2. _____

CHAPTER SIX

HEAL the Wounds

HEAL THE WOUNDS

Tip# 28   Forgiveness Frees You

You've probably heard that forgiveness frees you. Perhaps you've even heard that not forgiving someone is hurting *you* more that the person who inflicted the pain. The hard part is actually doing it. I did it and it took patience, soul searching and many prayers for strength.

It's tough to write about forgiveness, but I'll try. I want to help as many people as possible with this book and if you've lived with anxiety and anger for many years as I had, it's time to read on and perhaps heal yourself through forgiveness. It's not an easy thing to do, but I know that living with deep rooted hurt eats away at us from the inside. I believe that it might be the cause of many diseases and ailments that seem impossible to heal. If we are to move forward from the anger, hurt and feeling of helplessness, forgiving is one of the most *freeing* things a person can do.

As for me, there came a time when I was ready to forgive. One of those people I forgave was myself, since I allowed part of my life to live at the hands of abuse. There were many other people I met on my path who I needed to forgive but I'll just mention a couple...

    I grew up as a kid in the 1950s and 1960s. I know it was a different time back then, but my childhood friend would tell you that the police were always at our house for domestic violence. Alcohol was a big factor in my father's rages. I testified against my Dad when I was twelve because my Mom wanted to be free and divorce him. Unfortunately, she went back to him a few weeks after the court case. I truly don't believe he thought he did anything wrong. He didn't go to jail but he had restraining orders on him from hitting us. He was allowed to live under our roof and, unfortunately for us, the restraining order didn't seem to matter behind closed doors. I remember him saying to me that the restraining order meant he couldn't hit me but it said nothing about kicking. At age 12, I had a choice to live on the streets or at our house. I stayed home, but many days I thought the streets would be safer.

I forgave my Mom for going back to him. In the 1960s, divorced women were looked down upon and she had four kids to feed. I realized her options were few. I was the oldest and endured most of the physical and mental abuse. It would be a long path to forgiving my Dad.

A few years ago I was sitting beside my Dad as he approached the last days of his life. I had forgiven him 25 years earlier when my first daughter was born. I wanted her to know she had a grandparent (my Mom had died when I was in my twenties). He was now in his eighties and, although he was now saying over and over how he loved me, I never heard the words, "I'm sorry."

As I sat by his bed one afternoon I remember him saying, "I've been a good guy." He paused, looked at me and then said, "well, maybe I did a few *bad* things." That was the closest I ever got as an apology. I just nodded and didn't say a word. I noticed for the first time that the bubble of anger didn't boil up inside me. The need for a true apology wasn't necessary. I had forgiven him.

After he passed away, I was the only one with him until the coroner arrived. I blessed his soul and prayed over him. I could feel his soul surrounding me with light and love.

I followed the cycle, as most daughters do and I married an abuser. Many women repeat the generational path and pick a husband based on the traits of their father (usually without knowing it). I lived with him for over fourteen years and felt I could change him. Unfortunately, he chose alcohol over his kids and myself. I decided to change the direction my Mom took and I went to a women's shelter for abused women. I had a five year old and seven year old in tow. I divorced him.

My ex-husband was only in his sixties when he passed away. The coroner concluded that it was his drinking that killed him. I'll never forget the call from my oldest daughter, "I just found out that Dad died." My eyes filled up with tears. I still had love for him but he had a dis-*ease* of drinking. I cared a great deal but he couldn't and wouldn't help himself. I found out that he had not only abused me but also mentally abused most of his immediate family. No one wanted to pay for or attend a memorial for him. I decided to hold a get-together at my house for his friends, my daughters and myself. I set up all the beautiful photos of him and played some of his favorite music. His friends said a few words about the healthier younger man they knew and loved. I'll never forget my daughter saying, "I never knew him as those people spoke of him, thanks for doing this Mom." I had forgiven him years before and I knew that this was the proof. Ironically, both my Dad and ex-husband died within a few days of each other, in the same year. There was no carry-forward of anger, hostility or hurt. I had forgiven and it was finished.

Forgiveness also changed my view and memory of both my ex-husband and father. Now when I reflect back I remember my ex-husband the way he was when we were young and dating. These are the healthy and happy memories. Forgiveness has cast him in a new light. As for my Dad, I reflect on him lying in his hospital bed telling me over and over that he loved me. Forgiveness lifts us to another awareness. It's the most freeing thing to release pain and inner turmoil of anger and hurt and instead reflect on those good days.

As you read this section of the book, did someone come to mind? Did you feel the pain and hurt again? Perhaps the anger? After reading this is there someone you want to forgive? It won't be easy, but I truly feel it will be worth it to let go. Maybe you need counselling, more books on the subject or even prayers to give you the strength to get you through it. Ask yourself, as you approach this chapter of your life, whether you want to carry this burden with you into the precious years ahead.

If you can think of someone as you read these words I'd like you to just write a name below. You don't have to do anything about it right now but you'll know the name is there. Perhaps earmark this page and remember it.

I want to now wish you strength, courage, light and peace of mind. You've started your first step on the forgiveness journey.

_____

Tip#29   Don't Give Up on LOVE

As I mentioned in the last section, I had a rough first marriage. I'm sure many of you can relate. It left me somewhat bitter and disillusioned about finding another person but, I loved *LOVE*. The difference this time would have to be that I didn't get caught up in the whirlwind, the passion and the honeymoon phase.

   Before I could even think of finding *THE ONE,* I needed to take my time and be alone. I needed to get to know myself without a significant other. I also knew I needed counselling so I wouldn't repeat the cycle again and pick a man similar to my ex-husband and father.

   The good news is that all the counselling, soul searching and healing paid off. I found *THE ONE!*

HEAL THE WOUNDS

I met my current husband later in life. Our meeting had many coincidences, twists and turns. Here's our love story...

In the same town as the women's shelter that I had stayed at lived Bill. He was a single Dad of two young boys. I didn't meet him while I was in the shelter. I met him later after I had moved an hour away, to the big city.

Bill had spent about five years on his own after his ex-wife told him they were through. She went on to marry a co-worker. Bill had two boys aged four and seven and he had fifty per cent custody. In the 1990s, this amount of custody was rare. He was obviously a great Dad. He could have remained bitter about ever finding a mate again, but he too loved, *LOVE*.

Before we met, time was healing our wounds and both of us were starting to think much clearer. Pain and depression was making room for hope and happiness. We each decided to try this new thing called internet dating. It was 1997 and cost $950! There was a site that personally interviewed people and posted photos and background information on potential matches. This matchmaking program was not a program for hook-ups. It was for serious people who wanted to find love and long-term relationships. I was in my forties and feeling over-the-hill but I thought I could give this match-making thing a try.

     Bill and I joined the site around the same time. Then a funny thing happened. I had been on a few dates and started to get cold feet. I went into the matchmaking office to put my profile on hold. Suzanne, who worked at the matchmaking company, asked, "who have you asked to contact you"? I mentioned Bill's name. She got super excited and said, "You'd be perfect for each other!" Now, in those days, the matchmaking system worked by snail-mail (yes through the post office). The company would mail out the profiles of the people who you were interested in meeting. It had been about three weeks since I sent one to Bill, and he didn't respond to my request. I had forgotten that there were rotating postal strikes and Suzanne was convinced that Bill's request was lost in the mail. "I'm calling him right now!" Suzanne shouted. I was mortified and said, "NO!" The thought of Suzanne coaxing this *Bill* guy into seeing me seemed a little too desperate for my liking. I left the office... Suzanne called him. As Bill later told me, he did not receive my request through the mail and was thinking of dropping out of the program too. The reason he called me was because Suzanne said on his answering machine, "Bill...Heather's a lovely, lovely person."

 I clearly remember when he first called me. We talked for over an hour about how store bought lasagne is as good as homemade, and other random things. We were two lonely people who finally had someone to share life's little stories with. I remember thinking that we were talking like old friends. It didn't feel as though we were strangers.

We decided to meet for lunch and I knew that he could be *THE ONE*. He was a gentle man and was a great Dad. He also had two boys around the same age as my two girls. Could this be a perfect match?

He took me out on a second date to a movie. The movie was violent for a first official date, but that didn't matter. We had fun! We hadn't even had a first kiss during date #2. We sat in Bill's car and he showed photos of his kids. We treaded slowly on our soon-to-blossom love story.

Twenty-two years later we're still together and married. We're so blessed to have four healthy children that all get along. For those who follow me on social media, most of you have met Bill. Bill is someone I can just breathe with. We go on dates almost every Friday, even if it's just to a coffee shop. We built

HEAL THE WOUNDS

our social media and Awesome Over 50 business together and yes, he's helping me with this book.

    Try not to grow weary of finding someone to love who can truly love you back. We have our children, our friends and our pets but you if you can keep an open heart and an open mind, you might just find *THE ONE,* especially if you love, *LOVE.*

Tip#30   You are Worthy of RESPECT

If you haven't learned how to receive *respect* from others, why not start now?

Do you remember the section I wrote on *invisibility*? I talked about society and the way there seems to be a lack of respect for us older folks. Society is one thing, but what about the lack of respect by family members, co-workers and acquaintances? You know that these relationships and behaviors towards you are downright *toxic,* and have been for years.

As kids, for many of us, enduring bullying and toxic behavior from family may have been a necessary evil as we needed a roof over our heads. In grade school, many of us also felt the added pain of bullying from school-mates. As the years passed by, I became so accustomed to the lack of respect that I just decided to sit back and continue to allow some relatives and acquaintances steal my self-esteem. The bullying continued. Does this sound familiar? Well, guess what? You're not a kid anymore!

As the ones that are bullied, we've learned to take it on the chin, love them because they're family or long-term acquaintances, and put-*up* with their put-*downs*. The behaviors that are thrust upon us year after year are as toxic as salmonella or food poisoning, but its's a slow moving dis-*ease*. It seeps into our hearts, our minds, our body and our spirit and mucks up the essence of our true selves, the true *YOU*.

Every bully is different. Sometimes, they're just going through a difficult chapter of their lives. You bring your hurt to their attention and they get help or course-correct their behavior. Your wounds are healed. You need to have a good eye as to whether they deserve the label, *toxic*. However, if the behavior is never-ending and hurtful, it may be time to step back and step away. There are also scenarios where toxic behaviours continue because that person needs to recover from drugs, alcohol, or other addictions. Maybe they refuse to go to an intervention, because you'll always provide money or time which continues to *enable* them. It's a vicious cycle but *you* can take responsibility for your own well-being.

    I've had counselling for being an *enabler* and a *co-dependent* with my ex-husband. It was one of the best pieces of advice I ever received. It was a wide-awakening. I learned that the addict was not able to see me clearly and was instead projecting his own self-image of hatred and unworthiness onto me. Some people who chip away at your self-esteem (and your health) may not even have an addiction. They may want control over you or they might be consumed by ego. These are usually people who make you feel small. They are always belittling you. These behaviours are usually toxic.

    I won't say it's easy to walk away from a person who you know is hurting you, but it's easier with proper counselling. I haven't experienced this, but it must be very difficult if you're a parent and you have children who are affecting you. It could be a long road, but it starts with the first step. Sometimes, we can easily toss sour milk out of the fridge, but continue to drink in toxic flavors from a person who is constantly sour to us and has no intention to change.

    It took over a decade of abuse until I left my alcoholic ex-husband. I tried all the known ways to get him in to the 12 step meetings, but he shrugged it off as a cult. I was suffering and my daughters were suffering. I was also showing them that it was okay to be abused. I finally realized the harm I was doing to others and myself by staying in a toxic, no-win home environment.

    My ex-husband wasn't the only person I allowed to abuse and bully me. It wasn't until I was in my fifties when I decided that finally, enough was enough. I severed ties with everyone who had been throwing toxic muck my way for years. I realized that time was getting shorter in my life and I had a choice as to whom to share my journey with. I detoured from many acquaintances and relatives. It hurt my heart, but I had to move on to be happier and healthier.

    As I mentioned, my ex-husband passed away a few years ago of alcohol poisoning. Even though he sought some treatment after I left him, it was probably too little, too late. When I was with him, my health was disintegrating. By the time I checked into a shelter for abused women, I was on antibiotics. I was told to get counselling and rest. In the shelter I couldn't visit my friends or make calls to my co-workers. When I emerged back on the scene, many thought I was dead! Can you imagine? They didn't think I was on holiday or taking a break. I was forty-two, and they thought I was gone! When I asked them why they thought I was dead, their answer was, "you seemed so unhappy and unwell."

HEAL THE WOUNDS

Others can see your plight when you can't or don't want to. Remember, there are people out there who will respect you and truly care about you. Make some room for them in your life. Find help with a close friend or relative. I also urge you to seek counselling. Sometimes your relationship with a truly toxic person will change, but often it won't. Step back and step away. It's time to acknowledge the wear and tear it's taking on you.

    I have a saying, "we only have so many summers." Each day that we spend defending ourselves or engaging with toxic behaviour is wasted.

    If you're waking up to this message right now, I wish you the best. It's probably time to start on a different path in your life's journey. The new path will be much different but eventually you'll find self-care, self-love and the magic of *respect*.

Tip #31 STRESS AND WORRY are Silent Killers

It's not a surprise to read that stress and worry are proven to cause many ailments and indeed, in many cases are silent killers. It's a dangerous combo to your well-being and health for sure, but what if we shrug it off and think our ailments are just old age?

As for me, I was in denial. I used to get angry when people told me my migraines were brought on by stress. What a crazy diagnosis! Although I had been through acupuncture, homeopathy, naturopathy and modern medicine, no one could tell me what caused them. What imbalance in my body was making this pain unbearable? After over a decade of migraines (that showed up every few weeks) I couldn't find a reason nor cure. The migraines were beyond unbearable and I would lose about 5 pounds every time they emerged because I couldn't keep food down. The pain was excruciating. They lasted five to six days.

I finally realized it *WAS* brought on by stress and worry. Here's how I found out...

The days leading up to my wedding to my now-husband Bill, were stressful. I was so happy that I had just finished a migraine and another one likely wouldn't show up for a few weeks. I had invited most of my relatives to the wedding. My Dad wanted to stay in our home when we went away on our honeymoon. It was all good until he asked for my keys and wanted to drive around in our car. He had many DUI's and I knew my insurance wouldn't cover him. However, you just didn't say *NO* to my Dad. He eventually told me to stick my car up my ass and he no longer wanted the house or to attend the wedding. From there, it went from bad to worse. I remember holding the phone away from my ear as one of my younger siblings called me every name in the book. It was now my wedding day. I got a migraine. The stress and worry over a perfect day resulted in me barely able to see anything because of the pain. I was vomiting consistently.

Bill and I had planned a wonderful honeymoon at a luxury resort in the Caribbean. I can still hear Bill whispering in my ear as we approached the gate at the airport. He said, "try not to look sick or they may not let us on the flight."

I remember entering the lobby of the resort and apologizing to my new husband. I knew I'd be in bed sick for the next six days or so. Our honeymoon was one week.

We decided to find a restaurant where I could order soup and crackers to bring back to our suite. I still remember my wonderful husband saying, "It's okay" as I put my head on the pillow. He never left me. He went out to the open-air balcony to sit and took me for better or worse.

HEAL THE WOUNDS

I woke up a few hours later and believe it or not, I felt great! The migraine was gone! I knew it wasn't just the ocean breeze. I was content and no longer stressful or worried about all the things that could go wrong. I had just married the most wonderful man on the planet. My kids and his kids had now created a wonderful, non-toxic family.

    I'm no doctor, but once I let the stress go, I was healed. I decided to apply de-stressing and worry-free thoughts as much as possible after that trip. I applied it to both my personal and professional life. Today, I've been without migraines for years. I look back at that honeymoon as a turning point. It was my best medicine.

    This was an example of stress making one sick, but what about worry? Worry is the internal thought that tells you that a situation has impending doom. Worry is a just a conceived, fearful notion that something *might* happen.

I remember an old saying: "If you worry, remember that you might have to worry twice." This means that most of the things we worry about never happen. It's a waste to pre-worry. If a bad event actually happens, you have the right to worry because it's happening but pre-worrying means you worried twice. It's a long explanation, but so true. With four kids, I used to worry about everything. Now, I *"let-go and let-God,"* as the saying goes. It's trusting, freeing and calming, and I can use my energy to take action only where absolutely necessary.

Are you hanging on to excessive worry and stress? Think of some of your own ailments. Could less worry and less stress help? Why not take the time to work on it and find out?

Now that we're over 50, let's take these years that we have left with a little more spring in our step and a smile on our face. You can still eat your apple a day, but I truly believe that de-stressing and worrying less can help keep the doctor away!

Tip# 32   Learn to truly RELAX

How many of you feel that once you get away to that beach or go to the cottage, you can relax. Then, at the end of the vacation you decide you need a vacation from your vacation!

Maybe you're like me and never learned or participated in total relaxation. You didn't even want to learn because your life was in the fast lane and time waits for no one. I used to cringe if someone wanted to help teach me a new relaxation technique. I remember being a part of a Yoga class and falling asleep on my mat. That kind of relaxation in public I didn't need!

That was the *OLD* me. The *NEW* me is eager to tell you how my relaxation is going.

Up until about five years ago, as the expression goes, I was constantly "going at 110 mph with my hair on fire." I raised four kids, so multi-tasking was my middle name. I would spend most days working until 11:30 p.m. on our small business with only a small lunch and dinner break. This was the norm.

The turning point happened in the Caribbean in 2015 (our 3rd trip to Turks & Caicos). As we prepared for the trip, I recalled the last time my husband and I were at this exotic getaway. We went snorkeling, jet skiing, paragliding, etc. etc. We literally ran ourselves ragged with excursions and outings. On this trip, I had my carry-on and large luggage case. I had several outfits and even threw in a book (even though I knew I wouldn't have time to read it).

The moment I walked into our resort hotel room I felt something different than all the other times. We had chosen to upgrade to an ocean-front room. Once I stepped out on my terrace and the warm breeze hit me, I decided to take these seven days using my senses and not my busy-brain that always wanted to be entertained. I wanted to truly *relax,* but how to do it?

I had already given our hotel information to our kids and family members. Plus, I had placed all the emails to co-workers about our vacation. I decided to go old-school. I placed my cell phone into the room's safe. There would be no electronics on this trip. If someone needed me, they could call the resort hotel's front desk and we would be notified. I didn't take the cell phone out of the safe for the rest of the trip. Now, you might be thinking, "one week of no phone, I could never do that" but it's amazing how decisive I was! I remember thinking that checking it would be a weakness. I decided right then and there that busy Heather had to learn to slow down and relax. There was no how-to manual or video on how to do it, but there was paradise outside my window.

Soon after we arrived, Bill and I took a trip to a nearby grocery store. I remember we spent over $200 on groceries, plus rum and daiquiri mixes. Our room was an efficiency suite with a microwave, fridge and a toaster. For the entire trip, we basically just went between our room, the pool and the beach. Do you remember that book I threw in my luggage? I read it cover to cover. We had the best seat in the house. The view was breathtaking. We were in a low-rise townhouse style complex and our music was the soft breeze caressing the palm trees near our dining table. At the end of the seven days, we had re-kindled our love for each other as we walked for miles along white beaches. A couple of times we borrowed snorkeling gear and calmly swam with turtles and tropical fish but most of all, we learned the art of relaxation.

  I almost didn't want to turn on my phone when I took it out of the safe. I knew I had to get on a plane and leave paradise but I was no longer the Heather of the past. When I arrived home, I took the lessons learned and began to apply them to my daily life. This was the key. With the knowledge of *how* to truly relax, I could create my own sanctuary and paradise at home.

We're all different, and you don't need a vacation to get you to this point. There are other methods such as meditation, Yoga, Tai Chi, a good self-help book or counselling or classes.

If you've found how to truly relax, I applaud your progress. For me, the process is to put the phone away, turn off the T.V., sit quietly and breathe. Nature is always a great backdrop, but since I live in the city, I just sit on my bed with my Himalayan salt lamp glowing as my lemongrass essential oil diffuser fills the room. It's my little sanctuary area. The area calms my sights and senses and I do a form of meditation that certainly isn't by-the-book. I'm just kind of zoning out (or perhaps zoning *IN*) I'm not *doing* anything, I'm just *'being'*. Before I know it, a few hours have passed and I'm rejuvenated. I usually have my dog beside me and I think he's rejuvenated too! I also take many long baths (some with lavender bubbles) and I drift off to a world of de-stressing. There's another sanctuary spot in my yard under a lilac tree that provides just enough shade to create a mini oasis for reading.

These days, I also know that I have to prepare for my relaxation times away. I find that I need to set a few boundaries and prepare my mind to relax. I know that if I want to take some time off, preparation and scheduling any future social media posts and videos will have to be done before I leave. I know then that I can take many days off, as long as preparations are made ahead of time.

Recently, I visited my oldest daughter who lives in the country. It was my first time there and I found out very quickly how poor the WiFi signal was. Instead of panicking, I just relaxed. I had already pre-arranged most of the work I needed to do by scheduling videos and posts ahead of time. I could hear a little voice in my head saying, "you've got this." The world would still see all the videos and posts as usual.

HEAL THE WOUNDS

This freed me up for long walks and I was able to dine for hours with my daughter, laughing and conversing. I also took time to watch the rain dance on the greenery from her back porch. "What was happening to me"? Why, the art of relaxation, of course!

Cultivating a state of relaxation is one of the greatest achievements for the modern woman or man. If we can achieve stillness and calm and turn off our busy-brains, we can sleep better, be happier and healthier. We *can* make the decision not to let our modern-day communications rule us. We all have a choice. It's time to stop scrolling on our phones and find our serenity spot and breathe. If you haven't mastered it yet, isn't it time you began?

What are two things you could do to relax?

1. _____

2. _____

CHAPTER SEVEN

Wrinkles are your STORY-LINES

Tip #33   Talk PRO-AGE Instead Of Anti-Age

I always picture aging Grandparents with wrinkles. I just think that an elderly person should have wrinkles and a twinkle in their eyes. I won't be upset when my grandchildren point at my wrinkly eyes and ask, "What are those?" I'm not sure how they will react when I tell them, "they're crow's feet!" I think I found a new answer, and that's, they're my story-lines!"

There's a crazy thing I do when watching a movie. If a beautiful, older woman comes on the screen and has natural wrinkles, I'll say, "I want to look like her when I grow up." The future for me looks wonderful because I've seen it so many times before on the screen or on documentaries of famous women. I'm reminding myself that time is on-the-move and that we all can remain beautiful, just in a new form.

Now, having said that I prefer to grow old gracefully by no means says that I don't want you to be *YOU*. I've spoken many times in this book about being your authentic self. It's important, however, that you're not stretching your skin, getting needles or having face surgery because of pressure by magazines or social media models who are swaying you towards perfection.

It's a good idea for all of us to consider setting a new standard for beauty at an older age. An age that we can happily grow into. It's embracing what *will* happen instead of *fear* of the inevitable. I would rather call this time-frame *PRO-age* over Anti-age. Now, although I'm talking about wrinkles and story-lines *PRO*-age can also mean a lot of different things, but for this segment I'm just going to address the skincare and beauty side of things.

It seems to me that these days, the skincare and beauty cream companies seem to always be promoting anti-age products. Isn't that incorrect? If you're anti-something, aren't you against it? Now don't get me wrong, I'm the first one to rave about a new eye cream or neck cream that is making my skin smoother, reducing age spots or giving me a more radiant complexion. However, I'm still aging and I need more help with companies on my side for this process of the inevitable sagging and wrinkling of my skin.

Today, I'm seeing vertical lines above my mouth. I treat them with moisturizer but I know this is the beginning of sagging skin and the wrinkly texture. Instead of dreading my appearance, I think of how mature and lovely I will look with a full head of silver hair and my story-lines. My husband Bill looks very distinguished with his salt and pepper hair and laugh lines. We still think of each other as a great *catch*. Our aging hair and skin are signs of how many seasons of life we've been through.

I've added many new routines to my day over the past decade. Drinking more water, eating healthier, exercise, lots of moisturizer and practicing self-care to live a less stressful life help keep some of my story-lines at bay. I choose to wear fashionable clothes, love makeup, and still feel that I can rock a red carpet look. I'm *PRO*-age and feeling good about it!

My hope is that when I'm in my eighties, there will be many more naturally aging beauties who teach us about life lessons and what true beauty is all about. Wrinkles are story-lines and they are badges of honor. Let's remember that and wear them proudly.

Tip# 34   Ignore the NAY-SAYERS

I've talked about how people who try to take away your self-esteem can be hurtful but how do you proceed to ignore them, especially on social media?

If you're deciding to move forward with purpose and passion you're going to probably be out there on social platforms, on stage or just out in public. For most of us, we've had a long life of people voicing opinions on how we should act and look. It's always going to take strength with your reaction to the ugly comments and nay-sayers.

As most of you know, I post videos and images on social media to cheerlead the *PRO-Age* movement. Sometimes I will post with tag-lines such as, "Long hair – Don't care." This is where I get the most backlash. It seems that many people have an opinion on how a chin length bob-haircut would be "so much prettier" on me and "age-appropriate." They probably mean well, but I have been wearing my hair long for decades. It is truly and authentically *ME*. The comments that surprise me the most are when I post about how much I love my transition from bleach blonde to natural silver hair. I usually will post with the hash-tag, "Silver hair-Don't care." Many people mention in the comments that it makes me look haggard and old. When someone is not supportive and they make such a disparaging comment, it hurts.

Many people who are cruel with their comments on social media hide behind their laptop. They know you can't easily find them, so they can get their kicks out of saying whatever they want.

Just yesterday a wonderful woman that I follow posted a copy of a run of comments that were made after she was interviewed on a live media event as a 58 year old beauty. Some of the comments were mean-spirited and very hurtful. They said she looked like she was in her nineties and ugly (could have been the same person under different profiles). She became so upset that she told all of us that she wanted to take a long break from videos and social media. What a loss.

I kind of equate these types of comments with road rage. A person yells at you because you took too long to advance on a green light and they shake you up. As they leave a trail of dust behind, they know you are upset but somehow they feel superior and good about themselves. Their ego is beaming.

As you move forward in this chapter of your life, you will feel hurt from social media and others. You'll be tempted to change your fashion style back to all black and oversized clothing or perhaps get rid of all your makeup. You'll feel like you must look like the labels the cowards call you, such as *old hag* or *ugly*. Remember, it's not what they say, it's how you react. Learn how to just laugh and fluff it off.

Use the block feature on social media and don't bring those people back under any circumstances.

This is your turn to shine, but there are people out there who want to dim your light to make themselves feel better. As I mentioned before, they might even be your family or co-workers. Shine on anyway.

In the past, I used to read a mean comment over and over and feel bad. Then one day, I read a comment from a follower who respects me. Her comment went like this… "I'm so sorry you had to put up with that. The comment was so vindictive and mean-spirited. These people must be very angry with life. It's hard to ignore what they say. My empathy went out to you. How emotionally difficult it must have been but you have Bill and Hurricane to embrace you and make the hurt feel a lot better. If I was there, I'd make you a cup of tea and just sit there and talk."

Now, you may be asking, how do I remember every word she said"? Well... I have her response printed out and taped to my wall. It's been there for two years now and I look at it when the haters come out to play.

Whatever confusing comments or suggestions you've heard from others, take a deep breath and think before you react. Sometimes, it's best not to respond at all. Move on and you'll probably be reading a great, positive comment later. I've now noticed that my followers are all over a hater, I don't have to say a word, the people who respect me take care of things (*thanks so much for that)!*

Next time, try to pause before you get upset or even worse, change your plans based on their opinion.

Time will tell whether or not my 58 year old Insta-friend comes back to social media soon. Last time I looked at her posting she had 160 comments mostly from strong women encouraging her to move past these comments. She has a beautiful soul and we need her light.

This is a chapter of your life to shine! Be true to your authentic self no matter what others say. For many over 50s, it's about time!

Tip #35   Why not ditch THE DYE?

∼

So let's talk about the *hair and now* (pun intended, LOL).

Many people (women especially) are afraid that if they go grey or silver, they're going to look much older. The natural transitioning or grow-out stages can also be long and disheartening. No one wants to walk around with a skunk-like streak down the center part of their hair for months. I want to address these concerns in this segment.

Let's delve into the *looking older* idea by taking a stereotypical example of a distinguished older gentleman with salt and pepper hair. Most of us might perceive him as wealthy, wise and experienced in many aspects of life. Let's learn to see that in a woman with the same hair coloring. Fortunately, this observation and trend is growing. These days there's no such thing as the weaker sex. We've come a long way baby and we're spearheading companies as CEOs, directing movies, and are leaders of countries in the free world. If you're a woman reading this, embrace your distinguished look and wear it proudly. No matter what you have done for a living, you earned every one of those grey hairs, let the world know it!

Now, let's talk now about the transitioning and grow-out stages of grey or silver hair. There are many fixes for this. It will take a while to take the steps to transitioning, so know this in advance, when you're ditching the dye.

One of the choices for me was to get a colorist to add silver-all-over or do streaks. I had blonde hair and chose to add bleached out streaks put in to camouflage the white skunk-line as it grew in. If you have darker hair, you may need to do reverse black or brown streaks or resort to ideas that I'll mention later.

It took me about 18 months to totally ditch the dye and stop the bleached streaks. My hair grew out a lovely soft color of silver and I love it! Even if you're not happy with the result, you can always go back to the colorist. At least you tried.

There are other ways to grow out your locks. Some women cut off all their hair into a pixie cut or they simply wear wigs whenever they need to go out. Some also wear stylish headbands or scarves to hide their roots. These are all personal choices for women, and I understand it's not always easy. If you're a man reading this, it's a no-brainer. Most men just let it grow out and enter into that "distinguished stage." By the way, I looked up *DISTINGUISHED* in the dictionary and it read: "successful, authoritative and commanding great respect." I have to say that as a woman I've now entered into *MY* distinguished stage and I'll own that description.

I know that I'm lucky with my silver/grey hair grow-out but if you don't even try, how will you know if you will like your au-natural locks? Besides looking like your true, authentic-self, you will probably notice that this lighter color of hair actually allows makes your face look brighter. I changed my makeup when my new natural locks grew in. I needed less makeup and had an all-round glow. My hair was also now soft and silky and not damaged looking. If you haven't felt your hair or seen it without bleach or chemicals, you're in for a treat. Also, think of the extra time and money you will save by not seeing your colorist every six weeks.

Lastly, besides changing my makeup, I changed my shampoo. Ask your hair stylist about new shampoos and conditioners for your natural grey hair. Also, ask about the purple shampoo for grey/silver hair that you use every three to four washings. Get a good brand and watch how it helps your wonderful, natural shine.

I've noticed that the choice to embrace natural, aging hair could actually be a fashionable idea. At the time of writing this book, platinum silver hair was trending. Young women were actually asking to have my silver color!

I say, "ditch the dye and give it a go." I'll be waiting for you on the silver side!

Tip#36   Born to be ME

∽

We know that it isn't a good idea for teens to compare themselves to photo-shopped magazine covers, social posts and runway models. I believe that it's also a bad idea for us, more mature women and men, to try and look like the surgically re-designed celebrities, photo-shopped social media posts and to an extent, our twenty-something selves.

Since I'm a former model I've been around the beautiful people and actresses who have gone under the knife for breast implants, facelifts, and a nip and tuck. In the long run, as they aged, I found that many wanted the boob jobs reversed and they found the nip and tucks didn't last. As I said earlier, do what you want but *do it for the right reasons*. I urge you to also do your research on the cosmetic surgeries. If you don't find the right doctor, you may end up with a botched look, and irreversible damage or you could get an infection or something worse.

For me, I can't imagine myself with double D's or a frozen forehead. I went my entire modelling life not giving into the knife or needles, and I won't start now. This is my personal opinion, and not always a popular one, but I worry about what I would be projecting to my daughters if I underwent drastic cosmetic changes. Would I be promoting the idea that you always have to be changing your looks or re-constructing yourself so that others will accept you?

As I mentioned earlier, I consider my wrinkles as my story-lines and I naturally 'nip and tuck' my tummy into my stretchy jeans, skirts and shapewear. My body and face is constantly changing during the aging journey but thankfully, with a little makeup, skincare, healthy eating, exercise and self-confidence, I'm OK with the naturally evolving *ME*. I mentioned how my silver hair now lights up my face. I think Mother Nature actually knows what she's doing if we lean into the changes, but then, sometimes, we need a little magic of makeup.

I've been studying YouTube and visiting makeup counters to learn how to make-up my new droopier, hooded eyelids. I've studied how to get rid of my age spots that are appearing on my face and hands. It's a regular trek to the drugstore to find moisturizing facial masks as well as teeth whiteners. My approach is to grow old naturally with a little help from creams, lotions and makeup, but nothing that will distort or freeze up the true, authentic *ME*.

One day, I know the creams and makeup will no longer soften the sags and deep-set wrinkles that the natural aging process will show. But by then, I hope society will also change its view on aging. I'm seeing more and more grey hair and naturally-aging women on magazine covers, beauty ads and on social media. Let's keep this ball rolling! I hope we continue to celebrate the natural journey of us older folks, wrinkles and all. Accepting that silver-haired ladies and men with storylines on their faces are truly a thing of beauty!

My plan, is to be the true version of *Heather*, the way I was born to look in my aging years. Sure the creams will help but when I become a person in my 80s, I would like people to look at my story-lines (wrinkles) and see a beautiful, mature woman with incredibly white teeth.

CHAPTER EIGHT

You're never too old to DREAM

Tip #37 It's the JOURNEY, not the Destination

For many of us, we've become part of a society that wants instant gratification. Instant oatmeal, instant text messages, instant downloadable movies and songs. We get frustrated if something or someone takes too long. Some things do take time. In the case of *dreams*, they may take decades.

After age 50, most of the dust has settled from the hustle and bustle of raising kids and juggling jobs. Now, as you look forward, visions of old dreams may start dancing in your head.

Perhaps the dream is picking up a favorite hobby or skill you had years ago. Maybe you'd even like to build a business around it. Perhaps it's an invention, creating photography, painting or writing a book. Maybe the dream is just a personal one, such as a second home on a lake or in a warmer climate. Whatever it is, why not pursue that dream *NOW*?

I've found that everything changes when we start dreaming. All of a sudden, we're thinking of the vision and our lives take on a more hopeful and rosier view of things. We can start to enjoy the journey of life a bit more, through the process. Now your days are filled with excitement and learning. Your mind is full of endorphins energizing and keeping you feeling youthful. You are motivated to make progress. You're watching how-to videos and have never been on search engines so much in your life! You jump out of bed every morning and can't wait to be inspired with thoughts that will flow into your vision. You are dreaming of an adventure, a new path, a journey. The actual destination may or may not arrive (and that's the truth), but something will. The journey is taking you on a new, exciting road and you know you are a better person for it. You've started to grow again.

Along with these great feelings, we have another important one. Most of us learn by our later years to be *patient*. When you go towards your dream you're doing your research, survey studies and you vow to not give up because of minor setbacks. You are carefully getting your ducks in a row and you have learned not to launch your idea or dream too quickly.

Sometimes our goals are to help others and fulfilling the dream involves collaborations. Maybe you want to rescue dogs, launch a new leg brace invention or start a clothing donation service. Many times, you'll find that great minds think alike. As you put your dream out to the universe, people show up for you and your idea. This meeting of the minds helps to inject the process with new outlooks and turns wheels to make the dream a reality.

So what do you think? Isn't it time for us to embrace the next possible forty years and go for one (or some) of those back burner dreams, big or small?

We've been successful in many other things in our past, but many of us had small mouths to feed or other pressing commitments. Now is *NOW*. This world needs you. It needs another book that people are inspired by. It needs that breakthrough invention or creation. It needs your helpful idea that will contribute to a worthy cause.

In short, it's time to dust off your great idea and get it going before it (and you) rusts out.

Write down one dream you could start on. Take your time envision the process...

_____

_____

_____

_____

Tip #38 See it, then BELIEVE IT

So, you're now pumped up about your dreams. You're like an inflated balloon, you haven't tied it yet, but then whispers of doubt creep into your consciousness. Someone tells you that a friend of a friend tried a similar idea and it failed miserably (there goes a little air). Your best buddy who was going to join you can't anymore because his wife won't let him (a little more air). The doubt goes on and on. You haven't even started yet and already you feel deflated.

  The good news is that there's a buzz word around called *manifestation*. It's been around for centuries but now it's a *thing*. I truly believe it's not a bunch of hooey and I know for a fact that it actually works! It's all about envisioning the outcome. "I'll see it and believe it." Now, this is completely the opposite of "I'll believe it when I see it." Whenever that was spoken to me,

I knew it was a putdown. It made me feel that if I tried and didn't reach my goal, the nay-sayers were right and I was a loser. I don't believe that anymore. They can say whatever they want. I now *see it and believe it*! Yes, a belief has to be complemented with action but the belief is where it all starts. Hold the vision and miraculous things can happen. This is where vision boards really help. The image manifests in front of you and sets things in motion. I said that I know it works, here's an example…

    Bill and I hadn't been on a vacation for years. Day-to-day events made going on a dream trip difficult. We had responsibilities such as taking care of Bill's 95 year old mother, our dog, and the production of our YouTube channels. I saw the vacation taking place in my mind and decided to put it on a vision board. I looked at a photo of the Tower Bridge in London and the Eiffel Tower in Paris every day. I saw it and believed somehow we were going to get there. It's amazing what a little faith, belief and ingenuity can do. Bill's Mom got her care, my daughter took over our dog-sitting and we learned how to batch several videos and schedule them while we were away. We took a last-minute flight, booked our hotels and had a wonderful getaway in London and Paris for eight days. We talked about this trip for years but it wasn't until we cut out the picture of the Tower Bridge and Eiffel Tower from a magazine that I believe we manifested it into a reality.

As another example, it seems that my youngest daughter has a knack for manifesting. I remember in her prom year. She had seen a photo of a particular green dress in a magazine. This was before online stores were popular so we trekked around to prom dress stores in the city. Prom day was only a couple weeks away and I was getting nervous. In one store, they had a catalogue of fancy dresses. My daughter turned the page and there it was, the dress she saw in a magazine! She knew it was hers....but not so fast. The dress had to be special ordered and wouldn't arrive for another month. "No problem," my daughter said. "Here is my number, call me if it comes in." The sales clerk and I were puzzled. I wasn't about to put a deposit on a dress that would come in too late. So with no deposit, we drove home. I was worried that she wasn't going to have a dress at all. The very next day, the sales clerk called. She said she had goose bumps and was holding the green dress in my daughter's size! No one at the store remembered ordering it but somehow, my daughter knew it would turn up. She saw herself wearing it, believed she would have it in time for the prom, and manifested it out of thin air!

Do you remember my story of finding my first home? That was also about manifesting a dream. I've got dozens of other examples but what about you? Can you think back to when a dream became a reality? You could see yourself in your mind experiencing the outcome. Maybe it was something as small as pinning up a photo of the car you wanted, or the grade you wanted to get on a final exam. You may not have known it at the time, but you were manifesting and bringing your dream to yourself through attraction.

If you've got your dream in your head, start seeing it and believe it. Got it?...Good!...You're already starting to rev up those good vibrations!

Name something you envisioned and manifested in the past, then think of something you would like in the future...

Past manifestation:

_____

Future manifestation:

_____

Tip#39   Find the TIME

∾

So you're now in motion. You see the dream and you believe it, but remember how I mentioned that you needed to start to take some action? If you're going to do something exceptional in the next few years, you need to act. Why not start with getting rid of a lot of the noise, clutter and the routines that still surround you?

Here's a hypothetical situation…

It's Thursday night and you've finished your dinner at the usual time. Soon your favorite sitcom show will be on. You have the same after dinner drink in your hand and you might as well keep the T.V. on until the eleven o'clock news is over. The next day, you'll get up at the same time, go through your daily routine and you can't wait to see what happens next on your favorite T.V. crime show. Saturday is grocery shopping, liquor store and a few more errands. Then, you're finishing a wonderful dinner as your favorite sports team is about to play at 7 o'clock. Sound familiar? You may not think you're in a loop, but you are. If you're really going to follow that passion or purpose (and rock it) you need to break a few routines. Shake things up. Instead of that T.V. crime drama, sitcom, and other events that won't serve you, set that time aside to work on your dreams.

    I set aside my dream-accomplishing time each week depending on how much I need to get done. When I'm in-the-zone, I will sit on my bed with my little Yorkie beside me. I tell him I need my script-dog and he loves to snuggle for a few hours. As I write this, it's 10:48 p.m. on a Tuesday night. My husband has gone off to play hockey with his buddies (something he does most Tuesday nights). Unless there's a family function or the championship game for our home team, I'm writing. I'm in my room creating part of my vision for Awesome Over 50. I'm creating scripts and ideas for our YouTube videos and, in addition to the book, I'm writing for the newsletter, blogs and social media. My vision is a true passion and purpose for me. I really want to help others feel good about themselves as they age. I want to change society's labeling of us older folks so they see us as a generation making a difference and rocking this world. I truly believe I couldn't even find my purpose, passion and action plan unless I set the time aside to discover it.

Studies show that it takes about thirty days for regularly scheduled activity to become a habit. You can re-discover your passion, but you have to have action.

Before you know it, you could care less about that T.V. crime drama you used to always watch. Days take on a different dimension when you're following your heart. All you have to do is create a shift. A shift from distractions to attractions. When you're attracted to these dreams, passions and purpose time flies and the accomplishments flow effortlessly when you're in-the-zone. Relinquish those moments that no longer serve you and switch to something that does. Passion and purpose are not just pretty words. Incorporate them into your life and watch the awesomeness unfold around you.

List some possible times to schedule "Passion & Purpose" time...

1. Day of the Week_____

   Time:_____

2. Day of the Week_____

   Time:_____

3. Day of the Week_____

   Time:_____

Tip#40   START the Process

The time is now allotted. The visions are in your head and your Vision Board is on your wall. Now what?

These days, the dream-journey might start with your first internet search.

What a wonderful world we live in. We can easily read up on and learn steps 1 to 1,000 on how to create almost any dream we want. You just have to add a dash of your ingenuity and a cup of your creativity to the mix. Then bake for a few weeks or months. There are YouTube videos on how to create jewellery, do bookkeeping, create an online course, start a website or online store, or write your first book. With all of this at our fingertips, you'd think we would all get going on our dreams and goals? Sadly, many don't. Somehow, by the time many get to step two, they freeze. They start to second-guess. What will other's think? Am I capable? Can I commit to the process of learning all this new stuff? Our minds will be activated on so many levels. When going for our dreams, our minds are creating amazing things. Good things show up, but so do obstacles. One of the challenges might be our past patterns of thinking.

If the fear of failure has stopped you in your tracks, remember, it was Thomas Edison who said, "I have not failed, I just found 10,000 ways that didn't work." We'd all be in-the-dark if he (and *we)* gave up on those light bulb moments.

Remember that your first step doesn't have to be a giant leap for mankind. No one has to know that you're even working on your dream. I hardly spoke to anyone when I was writing my book. Only my closest friends and immediate family knew. I've learned from experience that I could trust them and they would be my cheerleaders. I also knew they would not set a time limit or unnecessary pressure on my journey. I could take it at my own pace. I knew that any outside external pressure, such as questioning when it would be released, would put a strain on my creativity and authenticity. The launch date would happen when it was supposed to. I needed to keep writing from the heart .Tell enough trustworthy people that have your back. That way you've started a commitment to your dream. You've made it real. A goal is a great thing if you think about it. Even better if you write it down, and the most achievable if you tell someone who believes in you.

    Once you get started, expect your journey to take all kinds of twists and turns. It's all part of the process. You might set out writing a novel, but then find yourself amongst movie makers and you're a script writer. You may decide to start up a craft beer business, but then find out about the rules and regulations and open a bistro with local beer brands instead. It really doesn't matter what your dream ends up looking like, as long as you get started.

It all has to start with step one. You still may have 999 more steps to go but go ahead and take that first step, your audience is waiting.

What could be the first 3 steps you could take to get started on your dream?

1. _____

2. _____

3. _____

Tip #41   History proves AGE IS NOT A BARRIER

One of your self-doubts might be that you're thinking too much about your age. Take that doubt away right now. There are so many inventions and businesses launched by people over 50. Could you imagine taking your pension money and starting up a fried chicken empire? How about taking a trip to France and then becoming a famous T.V. chef? Well, maybe with cholesterol counts and more people going vegan, the chicken industry and butter-heavy meals are not great examples for today, but the point is that history shows that excellence can happen at an older age. Get inspired and believe that if it happened for them, you have a shot at your dreams too!

Unless health is a deterrent, age is just a number. Think about the abundance of time you have left. Look back to when you were twenty. Think about all you've done in the last forty years. There is more than enough time left to follow your dreams.

It's funny how many people won't do something now because they think frailty in old age will happen sooner than later. Sometimes, we look at our parent's lifelines. My Mom died at age fifty-two. She developed brain cancer and it took her quickly. When I awoke on my fifty-third birthday, I was surprised that I had made it this far. You never know what tomorrow will bring, but I know for sure that today is a privilege. Let's live each day to the fullest!

I've seen documentaries on people in their 90s who still run marathons. I know women in their 80s who teach yoga. I'm still energized by people in Hollywood or in music bands who prove that you can still rock this world at age 70 or 80+!

Many people are living longer these days. We need to make our own history and we probably have more time than we think.

Forty years from now, I hope we won't be just looking at a man with a great chicken recipe as one of our few examples of people who started something later in life. It's up to us to show our future generations of aging women and men that they can be strong, creative contributors to innovation, causes, exceptional ideas, and a fruitful life.

Let's show the world what us Awesome over 50s are all about!!

Tip# 42   There's ALWAYS SOMETHING

As you move forward on your quest, there will be roadblocks. That's not a maybe, that's a certainty. In other words…"there's always something."

Perhaps you're just getting started and find that you've made too many commitments in your life already. Maybe the kids are grown but you're now the daycare babysitter for the grandkids for most of the year. Now, if this is your dream, that's okay and that's beautiful, but if you're finding that you've changed and you want to move on, you may need to step back a bit. What if you helped pay for daycare? What if you took the grandkids for a holiday in the summer to give the parents a break? Could you then take some time to do what your heart is calling you to do? Even a commitment to a neighborhood Pickle Ball team may have to be put on-hold if you want to start on your dreams.

There are many examples of these kind of commitments, especially if the world thinks you have already retired. Sometimes, we can't bring ourselves to express to others that we have new needs of our time. We're afraid that after we've mentioned it, people will put up such a fuss that we'll just say, "never mind, it was just a crazy dream." We've let people invade our space so much that we're all used up. Our brains are used to the same patterns. We give into their wishes and take away our precious time. Once again, we put our dreams on hold.

Now, if that's not you, that's great! I'm going to assume you've already cleared a path and have allotted time to move forward. Unfortunately, there still will be roadblocks. For everyone the blockages are different. Watch out for the fear-based ones or commitments that are draining too much of your money.

Remember that this is perhaps your last chance to make this dream happen. It's the final up-to-bat in the baseball game and you're up.

Whatever you do now means the championship. How many players have had that pressure on themselves and completed the base hit to bring in the winning run? It's not over until *YOU* say it's over. Watch out for your own patterns of fear and doubt, they'll make you weak at the knees and unable to step forward when you really need to.

Perhaps during the roadblocks you say, "it's just not the right time" The problem with this is that the time will never be '*right*'. You'll wait for the grandkids to grow up but then it might be too late. The world kept spinning, the years kept going by, but humanity missed out on your true, authentic presence. If this sounds heavy, I'm glad. Sometimes we need a kick in the pants to throw us off the never ending merry-go-round of self-doubt, obligations, guilt and time constraints.

If you have a big idea, a purpose for why you are here, remember that these are *YOUR* ideas and there will never be another *YOU* to fulfill it. Time goes by so quickly and if you blink, we all miss out.

**Tip#43   There's NO EXPIRY DATE
             on Dreams**

You're making headway and you're moving through the roadblocks. You now believe that a set-*back* is just a set-*up* for learning and you're getting better at what you're doing. You think you've chased away all the doubt and then it hits you…"what's going to happen to my dream, business or idea after I'm gone, or if I can no longer work at it"?

I have a few scenarios to help with this question…

Bill and I recently sold our gift basket business. We operated for it for over twenty years. It was mostly seasonal but there came a point where we knew that our path with Awesome over 50 needed more attention. We had outgrown the fast-paced nature of the Christmas gift basket season. I would stand on my feet for 12 hour days, for a full 6 weeks, 7 days a week. With no advertising our corporate client orders still kept coming in year after year. My conscience wouldn't allow me to say "no" to any of them. They counted on these end-of-year "*thank you*" gifts and I couldn't let them down.

  We finally decided one summer that it was time for our dream and gift basket business to move on to someone else. We put out emails and finally found a family owned business that was perfect. We sold the client list, domains and other particulars and knew this was a perfect match. We helped with the transition and even designed some of the baskets for their first holiday season. Our dream didn't die. It continues to live on. Sometimes you start your dream and you realize you've outgrown it. The original dream will never have an expiration date but sometimes, for you, it's run its course. If possible, let someone else carry on with your dream. Then, get excited, because it's likely you'll get going on a new creative endeavor.

On another note, what if you know you'll reach an age where you may not see the dream fully maturing? Perhaps you want to start a little winery and create a perfect Pinot Noir. As you look into the future, you realize that some of the wine won't reach its peak for decades. Does this make you stop and back-pedal on the idea? Hell no! Instead you push forward and dream about the fruits of your labor. Relish the idea that future generations will love and enjoy the grapes that you're picking today!

Great things can happen with a little bit of time. A while back, I visited the Notre Dame Cathedral in Paris, France. It took almost 200 years to complete. Could you imagine if the architect said, "nope, give me a smaller church to build where I can see it finished." We would never be able to witness this amazing cathedral. It is a work of art. Many massive churches and cathedrals around the world took several generations to complete. Most of the original visionaries and architects knew that their dreams would outlast their life expectancy. Their dreams had no expiration date.

Our creative energy can continue for decades, if not centuries, into the future. I can see now how Awesome over 50 dream of mine might eventually be taken over by a younger person who will outlive me. I'll be breaking off sections of my business to be carried on by others, and when I'm in my 90s there will be another face (or faces!) for the over 50 crowd. I don't let that thought stop me. As a matter of fact, I find it inspiring! My dream will live on and it will be bigger and have more directions than I can even imagine right now. As others with the same purpose and beliefs come together to help Awesome over 50s focus, the sum of all the parts will be an amazing thing. It will take on a vibrant life of its own.

Sometimes, you have a deep desire, a passion for what you're doing but the recognition just isn't there. I'm reminded of artists such as Van Gogh who loved painting every day but never knew that he was creating priceless masterpieces that would soon hang on gallery walls. If you're a painter, a sculptor, a composer or any other artist, keep enjoying the process, the passion and the journey. Mozart is another example of someone who pursued his gift but died impoverished. He couldn't, and didn't stop his passion. He was enjoying the journey. Now his legacy and music lives on.

Create, dream and leave your mark. Whether the paint is drying on the canvas or the wine is aging. Create your masterpiece for today and also for in the future of tomorrow!

CHAPTER NINE

WHAT'S NEXT?!

WHAT'S NEXT?!

**Tip#44   The Best Things in Life are
              NOT THINGS**

There's a trap that many dreamers get caught up in, and that's in finances and the stuff they hoped they'd get from their goals. They're loving what they're doing, they have a great following, but the mansion and fancy car have not materialized. If that's *you*, don't put the brakes on your goals just yet.

   Now, if making some purchases are aligned with your true self, go ahead! Be authentically *you* but I urge you to step back and ask yourself: what you are you consuming these things *for*? Many people are buying things because of deep-seeded wounds. Getting something new and perhaps *the best* helps them to feel better about themselves. Perhaps it's filling a void or making up for all the things they never had as a kid. Many can't even afford these things. They run into debt and are in an ongoing financial crisis. Even if they are successful with their dream, the hole might never be filled. The loops may continue from one financial crisis to another unless conscious changes are made. They've already become accustomed to a lack of financial stability and it now feels normal.

Ego can play a big part in consumerism and a lack of self-esteem. In both cases, the ego sees *things* as status symbols for praise and admiration. All of these issues won't be repaired with another purchase. The gratification is only fleeting.

I had my mad, greedy time in the 1980s. It was all about the right model of car or the right designer dress. When I fled from my abusive first husband twenty-three years ago, I walked away from everything. I left a 5,000 square foot custom-built home on a lake, a rental home that we owned next door, a boat, a luxury car and a convertible. My ex-husband was not capable of taking care of our young daughters as an alcoholic, so I gave him everything except for a few pieces of furniture in exchange for full custody of the girls. I remember him saying, "this is a great deal!" I also gave up my lucrative real estate career so I could find a regular 9-to-5 job and have weekends and nights off for my girls. I moved into a dingy two-bedroom apartment in the city. I had to roll up towels at the base of my front door so the smell of marijuana wouldn't get into our unit from the neighbors. The building was forty years old and the pool was un-swimmable.

I had next to nothing, but I was finally happy. I was free and my children were safe. From that moment on, all the *STUFF* I thought was so important was not important at all. I used to take my big real estate commission cheques and buy the latest and greatest toys for my kids that I thought would make me a good parent. I bought two new cars direct from the dealership showroom. It was all in an effort to fix a failing marriage that was destined to destroy all of us. The *STUFF* I bought was a momentary high that faded fast because of the underlying lack of self-respect, abuse, and a dysfunctional family. Through conscious change, I was now making time for my kids and watching them grow. It was magical.

Are you putting precious memories on the backburner so you can renovate your kitchen once again or search for a bigger, more grandiose house? How much of your time is spent searching and filling your life with *things*? What about all the time that you spend going to home improvement stores, designer clothing boutiques and other high-end stores? What is this taking you away from? Even the size of your T.V. can be a materialistic draw with consequences. What if you buy the big T.V. and decide to move so you can have a theater room? Do you see how we start down the path of more-and-more consumption and then have little time for family, loved ones or even to continue the pursuit of our *dreams*?

"What are the best *things* in life, really?" How about making memories instead of making new home theater plans. Perhaps traveling somewhere with the entire family instead of traveling to the car dealership. Creating a garden yourself instead of over-seeing the landscapers who are on retainer each week.

My wish is that many of you discover that a simple life is better. I hope you enjoy the flowers you planted in your garden and stop to smell the roses. Take the time to laugh out loud as you have fun with your grandkids or pet. Get rid of all the air fresheners in the kitchen and instead breathe in the aroma of chili slowly simmering on the stove. I hope all your senses are heightened as you put your credit cards and thoughts of buying the next big *thing* to rest.

In the 80s, many of our lives were spent in the fast lane. Let's slow down, spend less and truly accept that the best *thing*s in life are truly *not things*.

Tip#45   Keep EVOLVING

Sometimes, the ordinary and routine seem so familiar that we don't evolve. Studies have shown that many people who retire from their job still wake up at the same time every morning, well after they've said farewell to their morning commute. I'm not saying that waking up and eating your cereal at 7:30 a.m. each weekday is a bad idea, but are you capable of changing a habit if you needed to, or wanted to? So far in this book, there have been 44 tips and most of them involve embracing some kind of change. I'm sure you've found some interesting ideas to move forward, especially if you are near or in retirement.

Here's the definition of retirement: "the time of life when one chooses to permanently leave the workforce behind." That sounds rather, well, *permanent*! It also sounds somewhat sedentary. Our minds and bodies are not things to waste at any age. Studies also show that those who retire and don't keep themselves active have more health concerns.

Work is not just another four-letter word. Whether you're volunteering, starting a small business or creating your own art studio in a spare room, you could choose to be busy and working on something. Busy hands and minds keep us youthful, but we have to keep evolving. Routines of watching T.V. or going out for Saturday night drinks with the same old crowd each week may not serve your goals or even your health anymore. Remember the example in Tip# 39 on finding time for your dream?

Perhaps you did start on a dream and now it's time for marketing. You are in the habit of getting up at 6 a.m. and are usually in bed by 10 p.m. However, you might now have to go to events that involve after-dinner parties and get-togethers. How are you going to stay awake? Well, how about *evolving*! Most people who are entrepreneurs know that they may need to stay up until the wee hours of the morning and change their body-clock. As many of you can now work from home, you may not need to factor in that morning commute. How about getting up at 8 a.m. instead of 6 a.m.? You just added two more hours of awake-time to your evenings! Choose how you want to live your days, and adjust as necessary through consistent practice.

Whatever you go through, your future will probably involve some *evolution*. Tech, trends and time waits for no one these days. Try not to be a stick-in-the-mud. Instead of hoping the old ways will come back, think about flowing with the turning tides. It won't be easy, but if you choose to not *evolve*, you're just standing still.

Whether you volunteer your time, start a new hobby, small business, create your own art studio or follow that passion or purpose that has been tapping you on the shoulder, just keep moving forward. Use this new fire in your belly

WHAT'S NEXT?!

and the warmth in your heart to keep evolving towards a passionate, lively life. *You got this!*

Tip#46 Your EXPERIENCES HAVE VALUE

I guess by now you know that I (and many others) don't believe that Over 50s are washed-up or over-the-hill. If you've lived for more than a half century, you have a lot of knowledge. You have old-school ideas and a history that can still contribute to today's needs and into the future.

As I mentioned before, I spent many years as a real estate agent. Although times have definitely changed in this market with new apps and ways to create offers on our phones, I was often asked to speak in front of a group of agents and teach the new kids how to prospect and hold onto existing clients. My soft-sell approach to caring about buyers and sellers worked. I taught classes and gave speeches on putting people first and how the money would follow. I taught young agents how I set up an open house and how to stage a home that looks comfortable, clean and inviting. After my talks, I would always get a few bright-eyed youngsters asking dozens of questions. They knew that my old-school ways would be a great addition to their apps and new-school technology.

You may have a skill, trade, hobby or occupation where the basics still hold true. Don't put yourself out to pasture just yet. For example, maybe you know how to play jazz, paint a house or complete home improvements. Maybe you were great at sewing or knitting (that's coming back these days), or perhaps you're well-read on world history. Whatever it is, if you share it, people will probably still find it exciting or useful. You don't even have to turn it into a business. Maybe just pass on your experience to your kids, your young neighbors, or offer talks at the community center.

It doesn't always have to be a skill or a topic of interest. We can also pass on our life experiences. Maybe we helped raise a sibling with autism or cared for an aging parent. Perhaps you have cared for rescue dogs or cats.

Maybe you know how cook a great meal. These are love and life skills that need to be shared.

I recently read about a woman who passed away in a nearby city and when they went into her home, they found she had forty-seven malnourished small dogs. An outpouring of dog lovers offered to bathe, feed and foster a dog or two until they found forever homes. These people had no special skills except for having dog-loving hearts to reach out and help.

If we look around, we can observe people expressing and sharing their experiences. I've been to museums where the security guard will tell me almost everything about the dinosaur bones I'm looking at. It's a person who truly loves what he or she is doing and the environment they are in.

Recently I watched a documentary about a store that fixes and sells old typewriters. Old typewriters?! With all the computers and word processors out in the world now, why would anyone even consider a typewriter? The end of the documentary it made it clear that typewriters never corrected your spelling or grammar. If you were a writer, you could let your creative thoughts flow and the result was a piece of paper with your creative process on it. They also made the point that unlike a computer, the typewriter can't crash and take all your work and time with it. At the end of the documentary, I was amazed to see how many young people were jumping on this band wagon. The typewriter repair-people had old-school knowledge and it was valuable. Dust off *your* knowledge and find if it still has meaning in today's society.

I think there will always be a need for the experiences and knowledge of us awesome ones over 50. We're the people with decades of experience. The Mr. or Ms. Fix-its, the cooks who can make a meal out of a pantry of canned goods, or solve a business or family crisis in minutes. In most situations, there's an old-school way to work it out and that makes us a special breed.

Think of how you can contribute in the old-school ways because there will never be an *app* for that!

WHAT'S NEXT?!

Tip# 47   WHO ELSE is with you?

Let's delve into the expansion of the people you surround yourself with at this time of your life. Who are the treasured *'keepers'* of your existing friends and family? Who might be coming into your life?

As I've mentioned, my husband Bill is on a hockey team where many of the guys are over 50. Most of them are great guys that he's known since high school (what I mean by *keepers*). Every week, they go out for fun, exercise, and socializing. Most of them wouldn't miss those Tuesday nights unless there's an emergency. It's something they all look forward to.

As far as finding new, like-minded people, there are many options to meet new future friends with similar interests. I'm often asked to join a Pickleball team by our neighbors. It sounds like a lot of fun and, since it's a racquet sport like tennis, I might even be a good addition to the team. Most players in the Pickleball teams in my neighborhood are over 50 and although it's competitive, they play for fun and recreation. There are also travel tours where people join up year after year to travel to new destinations. They know the next tour may be Rome or Sydney, and they make plans so they can once again enjoy each other's company.

Some find each other at major sporting events, art exhibits, or are just great new neighbors. The list goes on and on. A friendship of like-minds is similar to when you joined a club in high school. Whether it was a band, an after-school team, a photography club, or helping a charity or cause, you felt great being together with like-minded people.

When it comes to accepting invitations or committing to a team, you may want to look for people who also go at a similar pace as you. Make sure you get the facts on competitiveness and their goals. Bike riding that turns out to be speed racing, or travel trips that include a trek to the top of Mount Everest, may not be something you want to commit to.

On the topic of pace, however, not everyone in your group needs to be over 50. Technology interests are a great example where you may be the oldest one in the room. It's the interest that you all share. Whether it's a new app or typewriters, age may not be a barrier to like-minded people.

I find that these groups are be healthy for me. Many times, we feel obligated to hang out with the toxic people at work or even some relatives in our family. Sometimes, it's great to have a fun commitment to go to and miss the office party or yet another family barbeque that takes up too many Sundays on your short summer schedule.

I think it's important, when seeking out new groups and friends, that you find not only like-minded people, but also people who give you a pat on the back. Folks who will boost your self-esteem and confidence instead of tearing it down.

However, don't ignore your true, historic friends. The *"keepers."* Those who have been with you through thick and thin. People like Bill's hockey buddies who pat him on the back for a great goal, no matter what team they are on. Healthy friendships are still healthy friendships, no matter when they were formed.

What are some things you would love to get back into or discover? Where could you find those like-minded people? The joy of today's technology is that you can look up almost anything on search engines and social media. You can find active groups and the over 50 teams in your geographical area.

WHAT'S NEXT?!

Some ideas to start your search:

- Tai Chi classes
- Tennis or Pickleball over fifty
- Travel tours for your age group
- Pottery classes
- Sewing or knitting groups
- Book Clubs
- Motivational or meditation events

What ideas would you add to this list? To find our interests, we could look back to what really revved us up in our youth and get back into that flow. We can also look at our short-term dreams and goals and find a group that's on the same trajectory.

Whatever it will be, sometimes it requires a great deal of thought and searching to find the right group of people. Then, before you know it, there's a meet-up time and you're there! Don't be afraid to try a couple of groups. Once you find the like-minded faces smiling back at you, it can be life changing.

What comes to mind for you? What groups could you join? Write down two interests or passions. Don't forget to do your research and find the right fit for you.

1. _____

2. _____

WHAT'S NEXT?!

Tip# 48   LOVE like a person in their 90s. Don't wait.

There have been many studies on people in their 90s who talk about their past. For many, they don't speak about the great things they did. Instead, they speak about regrets. What they should or shouldn't have done. Many of these regrets were about *LOVE*.

As I mentioned earlier, my Dad passed away just before he turned 90. I visited him regularly in his later days. He kept telling me over and over how much he loved me. I had waited for those words for a long time. As a child, as a teenager, and growing up as an adult, they never came. It was a waiting game and it whittled away at my self-esteem and self-worth. In his last years, he loved like an old person, a person who knew his time was short. I told my Dad that I loved him too. I have no regrets in telling him I loved him. I won't be 90 and wish I had said something.

Another common regret in these studies is *LOVE* won and lost. Many people lost someone because of a careless act or infidelity. Many hurts are hard to fix. If you're the "*hurt*" person, you need to remember that someone faithful, caring and loving is still out there. If you're the person who "*hurt*," maybe it's time to see yourself in the future and change your hurtful ways. For the people who still love *LOVE* and are hesitant about finding a new partner, don't let love forever pass you by. Remember what I said in an earlier segment - if you truly want to be in love again, take the time to heal. Get counselling if you need to, and keep your options open to finding love again.

Another way to love is to show compassion and kindness. For many, we were taught to never hug or show emotion. That's okay if you don't like that kind of closeness, but if it's only because that's what your Dad or Mom taught you, it might be time to step the affection up a notch.

WHAT'S NEXT?!

Lately, I've been going to a lot of funerals. I see people shaking hands and making small talk. If it's a relative of the deceased and a person I know well, I give them a big hug. Sometimes, they don't want to let go of the embrace. Many times, their tears are falling on my shoulder. Hugs carry a strong form of love energy. The energy expresses that you truly care. They can feel the empathy. However, some people are just not huggers. In many settings, I usually ask, "are you a hugger"? Only a small handful of people say, "no." That's OK, but secretly I hope they will someday find the magic in a genuine hug.

Self-love is another important thing to remember. Forgive yourself for those youthful mistakes. Maybe you were the one who hurt people but now you're a kinder, gentler, more empathetic person. Forgive yourself and love who you are *now*. Our failures turn into life lessons, and then we choose to make smarter choices and become better people. Time is passing by quickly these days. Let's repair ourselves and our regrets.

As you move into being a more loving soul, forgiving and maybe even hugging along the way, you feel the warmth openly and freely. It's there with our actions, words and outpouring of love and we don't have to wait until our 90s to feel it.

WHAT'S NEXT?!

Tip# 49   Embrace an ATTITUDE OF GRATITUDE

One of the greatest gifts in my life was hearing someone say that I needed to write daily in a Gratitude Journal. They explained that it would help me to form an *attitude of gratitude*. A Gratitude Journal does not have to be fancy or elaborate. I just have a spiral notebook like I did in high school. Each day, I write something, no matter how small, and regardless of the type of day I've had.

Once you start this life-changing journey, over time you realize every day has a gift. The journal serves as a beautiful reminder of the lives we lead and why we should be thankful. Some of your entries could be about having a great meal, or how your dog makes your laugh. These all accumulate into big deals. There is an expression, 'don't sweat the small stuff,' but we also shouldn't take the good small stuff for granted. How can you live a truly amazing life if you can only give thanks for the big things in life, or only around the table at Thanksgiving?

I remember one evening when I was having a particularly *bad* day. Almost every night at dinner, my husband and I raise our wine glasses and toast to something. This night Bill said, "to my wonderful wife who I love so much." I probably muttered under my breath, "*whatever.*" Things had gone so wrong that day that I hardly acknowledged it. I still had to do more chores. I felt pressured all day. By the time I got into bed, I was once again fretting over the little things that had boiled up throughout the day. I looked at my Gratitude Journal and said, "what am I supposed to write in here"?! I then took my pen and wrote, "I have a husband who loves me." That was it. Waves of gratitude poured over me. Somehow, the pressures of the day were washed away. I was now in an *attitude of gratitude.*

Perhaps it was something your kid said to you today, or a warm "hello" from a dear friend or neighbor. It's there, you just have to shrug off the bad stuff and focus on the good.

I write in my Gratitude Journal at night, just before I go to bed. It's a great way to calm my nerves and think good, healing thoughts before I go to sleep. I would much rather doze off in a happy mood than one of anger or dread.

Living with an *attitude of gratitude* also cultivates empathy and sympathy for others. This certainly needs re-kindling in today's world. There is no greater gift than to sit with someone you care about, whether they are celebrating something or hurting, and share in that space to lend an ear and support. It is easier to do so when you are grateful for what and who surrounds you.

It's too bad that gratitude isn't taught in schools. It's a catalyst for living a life of abundance. Being grateful for everything you have and going to sleep with a sense of fullness and happiness. That's rich.

Write down tonight's gratitude entry and rewrite it in a journal as soon as you can.

_____

_____

_____

_____

_____

_____

WHAT'S NEXT?!

Tip #50 ...and finally –
         KEEP IT AWESOME!

We're at the end of the tips! Let's now, altogether, with thoughts of excitement and joy say, **"Keep it Awesome!!"**

I hope this book has spiced things up a bit and revved up your engines so you can always have something to look forward to. Let's all learn from the past, enjoy the *NOW* and embrace our dreams in the future.

My wish is that you participate in many new facets of life and make yours more awesome with gratitude, exciting endeavours and embracing new experiences.

Remember that there is no one else on this earth like *YOU*. You have a treasure trove of knowledge and understanding that no one else has. You are a contributor. People need your secret sauce, your special lust for life and the way you can transform them. Shine that energy!

Please don't fade into invisibility staying at home and disappearing. The world will be less awesome without your input.

I hope that you will do some of the things mentioned in this book and you'll feel different. You'll love different and *BE* different. You'll make your way home one night from an event and say, "wow, that experience was amazing!" People will go home after the meeting with you and say, "wow, that was incredible!"

Remember to keep this book as a guide and reference, and don't forget to connect with other *Awesome Ones* on social media.

In closing, I'd like to say that I've had many lessons lived and learned. I poured my heart out with my stories, sharing joy and sorrow along the way. I wanted to be transparent to exemplify how I was moving forward and evolving to enjoy a more Awesome Over 50 life. As we share this journey together

WHAT'S NEXT?!

as a generation, shine your light, you beautiful, amazing one, and... ***keep it awesome!***

FOLLOW HEATHER ON SOCIAL MEDIA & OTHER PLACES…

Instagram.com/awesomeover50 (daily posts)

Youtube.com/awesomeover50 (self-care, beauty & fashion)

Youtube.com/awesomeover50Inspiration (travel, food, fun, home-life)

Facebook.com/Awesomeover50

Website: **www.Awesomeover50.com**

Newsletter:
Awesomeover50.com/newsletter

ABOUT HEATHER HYDE

Heather Hyde is an international social media personality. Known for her popularity on YouTube for her Awesome over 50 & Awesome over 50 Inspiration channels, she has garnered millions of views.

Heather is happily married and a Mom to 4 grown children and a spoiled little Yorkshire Terrier.

You can follow Heather on YouTube, Instagram and Facebook just by searching *Awesome over 50*. Enjoy!

Printed in Great Britain
by Amazon